"Nowadays we are looking for a new kind of leader that we do not know how to describe. Not a dictator, but not passive either. Relational, but not timid. Relentless with vision, but a collaborator as well. In *Leading in Disorienting Times*, Gary Nelson and Peter Dickens not only describe this new leadership, they take us through the journey to get there. From their deep and tested wisdom, in both ministry and systems, they display how to do this leadership amidst the unparalleled culture shifts of our day."

—David Fitch, BR Lindner Chair of Evangelical Theology, Northern Seminary and Author of *Prodigal Christianity*

"*Leading in Disorienting Times* will help leaders to nurture healthy churches and effective organizations in the 21st Century. Interpreting a wealth of contemporary literature on leadership through years of experience leading church and non-church communities, Nelson and Dickens show us that leadership is more than tactical and technical. It is relational and transformational. They encourage us that uncertainties and complexities can be places of possibility and vitality when Christian leaders are grounded in God's love and connected to the people they serve. This book can help leaders to thrive despite threatening changes in contexts, communities and world."

—David Goatley, Lott Carey Mission Society

"G.K. Chesterton was once asked, along with several other pundits, what book he'd choose if stranded on a desert island. While others chose classic works of world literature, Chesterton answered, *Thomas' Guide to Practical Shipbuilding*. Well, if you could choose one book to help you navigate the challenges of leadership in these turbulent times, you're holding it. It's wise, it's deep, it's simple, and it's workable. Unless you enjoy being stuck, buy this, read this, apply this: everyone will be happy you did."

—Mark Buchanan, Author of *Your Church Is Too Safe*

"Gary and Peter manage to distill theory from major works on this topic reinforced by their years of experience and high level of expertise ... The concepts are very relevant and meaningful across different cultural settings. The book speaks to my context in Beirut, Lebanon, as effectively as it does in other contexts. I wish for every leader at my seminary and at my church to study this book and be challenged and inspired by its content."

—Elie Haddad, President,
Arab Baptist Theological Seminary, Beirut, Lebanon

"Nelson and Dickens have brought together exceptional church learning and outstanding secular business learning and communicated insights for all Christians who have a servant heart and desire the application tools to lead in powerful ways in their family, church, and community in order to connect others to Christ. This is a must-read for all those who are seeking to have an impact on others for Christ through their actions, words, and deeds."

—Steven D Holmes, President and CEO, VerifEye Technologies,
Springfree Trampolines and Chair of the Board of Governors,
Tyndale University College & Seminary

"As someone who over the past 40 years has led churches, businesses, and international development agencies, I welcome a book that will get me beyond the mechanical models of leadership that are so common today and replace it with an understanding of the realities of leading complex people and complex organizations in complex times. Gary Nelson and Peter Dickens bring solid scholarship and decades of real world experience to this discussion."

—Mike Baer, President and CEO of the Third Path Initiative

"Leading in Disorienting Times hit me where I live! Nelson and Dickens artfully blend contemporary leadership thought, lived story, and the Canadian context. A relevant and timely contribution to finding our way as we seek to lead our organizations through difficult questions, challenged assumptions, and revolutionary change."

—Melanie Humphreys, President, The King's University,
Edmonton, Alberta

"Insights help us see more and go further than what we ever could without them. In *Leading in Disorienting Times,* Nelson and Dickens provide multiple insights and illustrations that help us see the terrain of the land that has so radically changed in our disorienting times. With a breadth that comes from divergent backgrounds, Nelson and Dickens provide compasses and outlines for the journey that lies ahead for all of us. Not only do they provide key markers for this journey, they do so in a format that is compact, concise, and highly readable."

—Jul Meldenblik, President, Calvin Seminary

"This book will disappoint readers looking for checklists and recipes. But for readers who want a book that will stir personal reflection and challenge them to integrate their faith and leadership journeys, this book will be a gift."

—Brenda Zimmerman, Director of Health Industry Management Program and Associate Professor of Strategy/ Policy at Schulich School of Business, York University and Coauthor of *Getting to Maybe* and *Edgeware.*

"Its great strength is that it delves into all the current discussions about leadership, but does so with rich case study illustrations. Throughout, it threads the theme of relational leadership that appreciates the complexities of servant leadership today. Its chapters on transformational leadership and complex adaptive systems are superb. These are issues global leaders are addressing, and often what is suggested can have toxic outcomes for the leader and the ministry alike. However, Nelson and Dickens lead the reader forward in a nuanced and creative way."

—Ross Clifford, Principal, Morling Theological College, Sydney, Australia

"Some people see leadership as it was in former times. Some see it as it is today. Most important is seeing leadership as it is becoming. This future orientation calls for comfort with the concept of chaordic, which is the simultaneous existence of chaos and order. No one has a crystal clear view of future leadership. It is something we must live into with great wisdom and then appropriately reflect on what we have experienced. Yet there are values that characterize future leadership. The deepest core value is a sense of calling—especially a spiritual calling—to leadership. Nearby is having a passion for something for which leadership is being expressed—a church or other organization. Essential is insightful awareness of the times in which leadership is being provided. In *Leading in Disorienting Times* Gary Nelson and Peer Dickens help us navigate a journey involving all three of these values."

—George Bullard, President of The Columbia Partnership and General Secretary of the North American Baptist Fellowship

"Most of my life has been spent working with younger leaders and those who inspire, encourage, and serve them. I love their passion, vision, and deep desire to be a transformative and redemptive presence in the midst of constant change and a profoundly complex and uncertain world. But how they see it playing out in the midst of the challenges that they face is where vision and reality often collide and go their separate ways. What Nelson and Dickens have deftly achieved through a rich blend of theory, praxis, and their own personal stories and leadership experiences is the provision of a hopeful relational framework for fresh structures and processes to emerge and to bring purpose and rootedness to leading in disorienting times. High value for all leaders."

—John H. Wilkinson, Executive Coach and Strategist, Youth Unlimited Toronto / Youth For Christ Canada

"Navigation using the maps of the past is uncertain at best and perilous at worst in a world where the landscape is in a state of continuous and disorienting change. Thankfully, Dickens and Nelson have leveraged their combined and proven leadership experience to provide a steadfast compass that will help leaders wisely and practically pilot their organizations into the future."

—Steve Brown, President, Arrow Leadership and Author of *Leading Me*

"Managerial leadership, the authors insist, will serve adequately neither our churches nor our social institutions in a world of accelerating complexity. The renewing change so urgently required of our churches and societal institutions in post-Christendom culture requires biblically and contextually informed changes of leadership disposition, vision, relational commitments, and motivational instincts—nothing short of comprehensive leadership re-imagination. I savor the prospect of sharing it with my students and colleagues in biblical higher education leadership."

—Ralph E. Enlow, Jr. President of the Association
for Biblical Higher Education

"This book gives voice to things that many leaders in our generation feel and live. It offers earthly inspiration to keep engaged with transition in order to facilitate transformation. The authors' refreshing take on contemporary leadership encourages us to know that in the midst of cultural disorientation, we are not left without compass or companions."

—Anna Robbins, Acadia Divinity College

"Peter Dickens and Gary Nelson have articulated, effectively, the concept that leadership is well-advised to think of organizations as living organisms rather than machines. They have applied their respective experiences in the world of health care (Dickens) and the church (Nelson). In so doing, they enunciate the complexity of organizations and the multi-dimensional cross-hatching of the systems within which these organizations exist. Out of these considerations we learn of the ways by which leaders can encounter and creatively reshape the worlds in which organizations exist."

—Lloyd Mackey, Canadian Journalist

"This book captures the reality of leadership today and the challenges we face in order to navigate our ambiguous future while remaining committed and passionate in God's mission. With authentic experience, sensitivity, and wisdom, it serves as a guide to promote the adaptive and continuous dialogue leaders need. Like a map it points out where you are, where you want to be, and the areas you want to avoid. Eminently practical."

—Stacey Campbell, CEO, Prison Fellowship Canada

"One of the biggest ideas in this book is the wake-up call for leaders to focus their goals on the overarching question, what kind of organization do we want to be? Purpose, not programs, is what drives Gary and Peter to give us the best of their leadership advice in this gutsy book. It's a great reboot from seasoned experts who lead in a daunting field of faith for all, versus the zeitgeist of individualized secularization."

—Lorna Dueck / Context TV President, *Globe* and *Mail* Commentary Writer

"*Leading in Disorienting Times* highlights how the western world is careening towards a new and mostly unknown cultural shift. Demonstrating a strong grasp of the upcoming changes that are bewildering most in the church, Gary Nelson and Peter Dickens frame the issues with helpful language and concepts that provide a personal, practical, and insightful introduction regarding the kind of leadership that will be needed to navigate the future."

—Bruxy Cavey and Tim Day, The Meeting House

"Nelson and Dickens have created a wonderful amalgam that reinterprets Christian doctrine through the lens of leadership theory, and leadership theory through Christian doctrine. A marvelous example is their treatment of servant leadership, a theory of leadership that arguably has been misinterpreted more than any other. Nelson and Dickens, through their exegesis of the teachings of Jesus, give servant leadership a power and nuance that has been missing in most scholarly literature. I recommend this book, not just to church leaders, but to charitable and nonprofit organizations everywhere, whether faith-based or not."

—Jon F. Wergin, Antioch University

Leading in Disorienting Times

Key Leadership Resources from www.TCPBooks.info

George W. Bullard Jr.
Every Congregation Needs a Little Conflict
FaithSoaring Churches
Pursuing the Full Kingdom Potential of Your Congregation

Richard L. Hamm
Recreating the Church

Edward H. Hammett
Recovering Hope for your Church:
Moving beyond Maintenance and Missional to Incarnational Engagement

Making Shifts without Making Waves:
A Coach Approach to Soulful Leadership

Reaching People under 40 while Keeping People over 60:
Being Church to All Generations

Spiritual Leadership in a Secular Age:
Building Bridges Instead of Barriers

Gregory L. Hunt
Leading Congregations through Crisis

Cynthia Woolever and Deborah Bruce
Leadership That Fits Your Church:
What Kind of Pastor for What Kind of Congregation

The Sustaining Pastoral Excellence Peer Learning Team
So Much Better:
How Thousands of Pastors Help Each Other Thrive

Larry McSwain
The Calling of Congregational Leadership:
Being, Knowing, Doing Ministry

For more leadership resources, see
www.TheColumbiaPartnership.org
www.TCPBooks.info

Leading in Dis◉rienting Times

Navigating Church & Organizational Change

Gary V. Nelson and Peter M. Dickens

Copyright ©2015 by Gary Nelson and Peter Dickens.

All rights reserved. For permission to reuse content, please contact Copyright Clearance Center, 222 Rosewood Drive, Danvers, MA 01923, (978) 750-8400, www.copyright.com.

Bible quotations, unless otherwise noted, are from the *New Revised Standard Version Bible,* copyright 1989, Division of Christian Education of the National Council of the Churches of Christ in the United States of America. Used by permission. All rights reserved. **Scripture quotations marked (NIV)** are taken from the HOLY BIBLE, NEW INTERNATIONAL VERSION®. NIV®. Copyright © 1973, 1978, 1984 by International Bible Society. Used by permission of Zondervan Publishing House. All rights reserved. **Scripture marked NASB** is taken from the *NEW AMERICAN STANDARD BIBLE ®,* © Copyright The Lockman Foundation 1960, 1962, 1963, 1968, 1971, 1972, 1973, 1975, 1977, 1995. Used by permission. **Scripture marked TNIV** is taken from the HOLY BIBLE, TODAY'S NEW INTERNATIONAL VERSION®. TNIV®. Copyright © 2001, 2005 by International Bible Society. Used by permission of Zondervan. All rights reserved worldwide

Cover art: Depositphotos and Shutterstock.
Cover design: Scribe, Inc.

www.TheColumbiaPartnership.org
www.TCPBooks.com

PRINT: 9780827221765   EPUB: 9780827221772   EPDF: 9780827221789

Library of Congress Cataloging-in-Publication Data

Nelson, Gary Vincent, 1953-

  Leading in disorienting times : navigating church and organizational change / Gary V. Nelson, Peter M. Dickens ; foreword by Brenda Zimmerman—First [edition].

  pages cm

  ISBN 978-0-8272-2176-5

1. Christian leadership. 2. Church management. 3. Change—Religious aspects—Christianity. 4. Leadership. 5. Management. 6. Organizational change. I. Title.

BV652.1.N395 2015

253—dc23

2014047552

Contents

Acknowledgments

Gary's

Almost everything that I have learned about leadership I learned from my mentor, friend, and former colleague, George Baxter, at First Baptist Church in Regina, Saskatchewan. After studies at Fuller Seminary, I served under his mentorship for five years. George taught and modeled more about leadership in those years together than I have gleaned from any of my readings. In fact, most of my learning from reading the books on leadership came as "ah-ha" experiences, realizing that the authors were simply putting words to themes George had already pointed me toward. George, thank you.

This book is the fourth book I have written. Some have been collaborations with other writers. One constant in each project has always been my best friend and the love of my life, Carla. She has been the muse and the counterpoint to everything that I have ever put on page. In this particular book, as Peter and I had to navigate Peter's illness, she has played a more vital role than ever before. Thank you, Carla, for giving yourself so willingly to the task of taking what I write and making it better.

I also wish to acknowledge the places in which my leadership has been offered and received. First Baptist Church Edmonton, Canadian Baptist Ministries, and now, Tyndale University College & Seminary, have provided a fertile place for growth. You have affirmed me in what we felt called to do together. You are also the communities that have suffered through my growing pains.

Steve Holmes, in this current season of challenge, has become a friend as well as the chair of the Board of Tyndale. Thank you, Steve, for being a sounding board and a catalyst as we learn together what leadership is all about.

And to Peter, I honor your wisdom and friendship.

Peter's

I am deeply grateful to my colleague and friend, Gary, for inviting me into this project. In many ways, the ideas in this book have been swirling around in my head waiting not only for the opportunity, but for the wisdom of Gary and Carla to get the ideas into a useable form. I will always be grateful.

So many have influenced me on my exploration of complexity over the last 20 years, but I am particularly grateful to three people. Brenda Zimmerman, a leading authority on complexity in healthcare, was a mentor, friend, and colleague for 15 years. She pushed my thinking to levels I never could have taken it. Mike Baer, my oldest living friend and my spiritual companion, helped me see the works of God in this emerging science so that I could fully reconcile all of my thinking. Jon Wergin, my dissertation chair, was a brilliant sounding board and challenger, forcing me to a requisite level of rigor and discipline I would never have achieved on my own. Thank you, all!

On a personal note, I am grateful to my four amazing daughters who have honored my pursuits while only nominally trying to understand what I was talking about. Thank you, ladies. And my Marion: my love, my life, my muse, and my brilliant business partner. You are everything to me, my love. This book is for you.

Editor's Foreword

Inspiration and Wisdom for
21st-Century Christian Leaders

You have chosen wisely in deciding to read and learn from a book published by TCP Books from The Columbia Partnership.

We publish for

- Congregational leaders who desire to serve with greater faithfulness, effectiveness, and innovation.
- Christian ministers who seek to pursue and sustain excellence in ministry service.
- Members of congregations who desire to reach their full kingdom potential.
- Christian leaders who desire to use a coach approach in their ministry.
- Denominational and parachurch leaders who want to come alongside affiliated congregations in a servant leadership role.
- Consultants and coaches who desire to increase their learning concerning the congregations and Christian leaders they serve.

TCP Books is a sharing knowledge strategy of The Columbia Partnership, a community of Christian leaders seeking to transform the capacity of the North American Church to pursue and sustain vital Christ-centered ministry.

Primarily serving congregations, denominations, educational institutions, leadership development programs, and parachurch organizations, TCP also seeks to connect with individuals, businesses, and other organizations seeking a Christ-centered spiritual focus.

We welcome your comments on these books, and we welcome your suggestions for new subject areas and authors we ought to consider.

George Bullard, Senior Editor, TCP Books
The Columbia Partnership
332 Valley Springs Road, Columbia, SC 292236934
Voice: 803.622.0923, Website: www.TheColumbiaPartnership.org

Foreword

Our deepest fear is not that we are inadequate. Our deepest fear is that we are powerful beyond measure. It is our light, not our darkness, that most frightens us. We ask ourselves, who am I to be brilliant, gorgeous, talented fabulous? Actually, who are you not to be?...Your playing small does not serve the world. There's nothing enlightened about shrinking so that other people won't feel insecure around you. We are all meant to shine, as children do… It is not just in some of us; it is in everyone. And as we let our own light shine, we unconsciously give other people permission to do the same. As we are liberated from our own fear, our presence automatically liberates others.

–MARIANNE WILLIAMSON,
A RETURN TO LOVE: REFLECTIONS ON THE PRINCIPLES OF "A COURSE IN MIRACLES"

Marianne Williamson's words remind us of the profound paradoxes of leadership. Leadership as a practice is about shining our own light on the world and if done so with deep humility and authenticity, it creates opportunities for others to shine. Leadership is deeply personal and highly relational. It is not about shrinking or playing small but neither is it about hubris or arrogance. And fundamentally it is about love.

In *Leading in Disorienting Times* Gary Nelson and Peter Dickens engage in a dialogue about leadership and love. Their exploration of love is derived not from romantic notions but from the profound love demonstrated by God. They draw from their Christian faith to explore how we are to "mirror [God's] love back into the world through acts of service, sacrifice and even in our leadership." Their leadership is their act of Christian witness–an embodiment of their faith.

The book is written with a weave between leadership theories, Christian faith, and practical examples and stories from the authors' own leadership journeys in a variety of organizations. Both men have thought deeply about servant leaders and draw wisdom from their lived experience, thoughtful observations, and reflections on conceptual material. They model for us the power of reflection as they explore their failures, not as points of shame but as moments for learning.

Conceptually, the book draws heavily on ideas from complexity science. The authors express their frustration with traditional leadership theories as not being rooted in reality–in particular the reality of leading churches and faith-based organizations. Complexity science too has its roots in frustration. In the past thirty years, scientists in a wide range of disciplines have argued that the theories on which their discipline stands are deeply flawed or at least missing key insights. The theories were more about how we thought things should be rather than about the messy reality of how things actually behave. Complexity science tries to reconcile the messiness of life with all its idiosyncrasies and locally specific knowledge with the profound generalizability of wisdom of the ages. It is this dance of the particular and the general that intrigues the authors and gives them understanding.

The theories behind the book are nuanced and not easy to grasp for many who prefer checklists and recipes for leadership. This book will disappoint readers looking for such checklists and recipes. But for readers who want a book that will stir personal reflection and challenge them to integrate their faith and leadership journeys, this book will be a gift.

Brenda Zimmerman,
Schulich School of Business,
York University
October 2014

This book is dedicated to Brenda Zimmerman, a friend and mentor, who passed away suddenly December 17, 2014.

1

Re-Imagining Leadership

We are entering, in short, a revolutionary age. And we are doing so with ideas, leaders, and institutions that are better suited for a world now several centuries behind us.
—JOSHUA COOPER RAMO, THE AGE OF THE UNTHINKABLE

"Virtually everything our modern culture believes about the type of leadership required to transform our institutions is wrong. It is also dangerous."[1] This is what Jim Collins, the organizational management guru, believes. We think he may be right. After all, we have been hoarding leadership books for years and usually have one or two of them lying on our bedside tables for future reading. We are, however, practitioners, and sometimes, after we have read a book on leadership, we wonder if some of these writers have ever led a congregation or an organization; if they have ever worked out their theories in a context other than the one about which they have written. Theories are great, but the reality is that they have to be lived out in the hothouse of real people working to accomplish the mission their organizations exist to fulfill.

That is why we decided to write this book. We have lived out a sense of call to leadership in a variety of settings. In each we have been tested, and the various theories we attempted to implement have been challenged. Each time we have learned to rely on some key ideas and themes. We propose that leadership is not as complicated as the books have made it; nor is it as simple as implementing a few magic steps. Like the threads woven together in a tapestry, we have been able to identify a collection of themes that resonate as true and practical within the leadership challenges we each have been given.

Peter's Background

Twenty years ago, Peter was faced with a challenge. After several years in increasingly senior management roles being in charge of large divisions and holding enormous responsibilities, he decided to strike out on his own and develop a consultancy that would focus on strategic planning and developing the leadership capacity needed to drive those plans. As he moved away from senior leadership, Peter closely held several lessons he had learned, one of which was that he came to know that good plans are focused on a clearly defined goal or goals and an articulated detailed implementation plan to attain them.

He began his consultancy by coming alongside clients to help them develop what became highly prescriptive plans. They could have been sold by the pound because their value was their weight, not their clarity. However, Peter did not settle there. After the plans had been developed, he worked to enhance the capacity of the senior organizational leaders who would be tasked to manage the change and keep the organization focused on these "weighty" initiatives.

To his utter surprise and to that of his clients, the plans did not work! Unpredictability had crept in. All the well-crafted goals and objectives seemed to lead to dead-ends or down pointless rabbit trails. Unfortunately, the response was always to go back to the fancy retreat center and do it all over again: another brilliant idea, another similar result.

During this period, Peter and his clients began to realize that their deepest beliefs about organizational success were flawed. They began to sense that the root of the problem was foundational. They had believed, as had thousands before them, that organizations ran like a machine. The leader's job was to plan carefully and manage the flawless execution they had designed. If it did not work, the response was to reengineer the organization or, worse, just work harder. They tenaciously held to the belief that the problem was not in the plan or even in the implementation. It had to be the people. These conclusions led to embracing management by objectives and enhanced training. After all, Henry Ford is often credited with saying, "All I wanted was their hands and I got the whole damn body." If the plan and execution are not producing results, we need to find a way to motivate people differently.

Peter gradually came to the conclusion that the fatal flaw lay much deeper. The assumptions about effectiveness and the view of people needed to be challenged. People are not machines. They are living, changing, adapting organisms that come together in sometimes unpredictable ways and produce surprising results.

In the meantime, in the larger discussion about organizations and leadership, many of the most respected thinkers began writing about organizations in very different ways. Borrowing from a range of sciences–from quantum math, physics and biology, economics and sociology–they explored this curious area of study called chaos theory. For some, the science sounded murky but the underlying themes and foundational presuppositions were fascinating.

Peter began to imagine a different way of thinking about organizations–not as machines but more like ecosystems of people. This approach would emerge and become framed around the organizational change language that was becoming known as complex adaptive systems. At its beginning was a revolutionary starting point that demanded the challenge of needing to learn new functional skills. At a deeper level, it meant engaging in the hard process of changing foundational beliefs and narratives about virtually everything we have long held to be true. People like Jack Mezirow and others suggest that this kind of learning–what they call transformative learning–begins with a disorienting dilemma. A leader of a mission organization realizes that ease of travel to global destinations challenges the way that mission is perceived and ultimately acted out. A nation once able to sit aloof from the terror and destruction of an African disease, such as Ebola, now realizes that it is no longer isolated and safe.

Every person, by choice or circumstance, faces the opportunity to disassemble the mental models and assumptions with which one's sense of the world is made. It is never easy, and it demands a critical rethinking of the underpinnings of everything held dear. It allows for the possibility of having been wrong or of having held a misleading or false presupposition. We believe that the current times present leaders with such disorienting dilemmas on a daily basis. Our hope, therefore, is to reorient leaders to a way of thinking that offers possibilities for seeing their roles and tasks in new ways. It is this hope that has prompted the title of our book.

In the midst of all of this learning, Peter received a call from a former client. This client had just been appointed CEO of a suburban hospital that had been created out of the forced merger of two long-established community hospitals. No one in the two hospitals had expected the merger, and few had welcomed it. The government had mandated it, however, and so there was no option. The client invited Peter to be part of this process. Peter was intrigued. His consulting practice was thriving, and he had little interest in a "real job." Still, his friend was quite persuasive coaxing him to at least explore the possibilities.

Years later, this client admitted that his primary memory of Peter was as the "chaos guy." He did not really understand what that meant, but in facing the challenge of this forced merger, he wondered if Peter's radical views on how to transform an organization might work.

Peter was persuaded to join the executive team in the unheard of role of Vice President of Organization Development. His sole responsibility was to help create an innovative and agile culture across the organization that was significantly greater than the sum of its parts. Maybe it was ignorance or arrogance that caused him to leap at the chance, but this would be the largest canvas Peter would ever want in order to paint something significant and dramatic.

He did not really think much about the very clear possibility that his approach would not work. Isn't it fascinating how confident we are when we are younger? Instead, equipped with the nascent lessons learned about complexity theory and its application to organizational change, he joined the team.

Amazingly, the combination of collaborative and creative efforts of a great many people worked. It was not because they had all the right answers from the beginning, but because, in true emergent change style, the organization equipped itself to change quickly. They were able to stop doing the things that were not working well so they could focus on what was. Together, they journeyed in change and transition.

The results were dramatic. Within three years, the hospital was named one of the "Top 100 Employers" and accreditation reports lauded the culture of the organization. Financial and clinical performance, which had always been in the hands of extremely capable people, flourished as they embraced and were encouraged in what they were trying to do with the culture.

Gary's Background

Gary's learning has been shaped from a number of different experiences. His pastoral leadership has taken him from Canada to California and back again, and from staff ministry contexts to lead pastoral roles. For a period of time he served as a founding director of a post-graduate ministry formation program that sought to develop leadership for the changing urban environment in North America and around the world. In those years, he watched as some of the graduates of that program moved into settings that were just not ready for the change that needed to take place. He also began to realize that some organizations are willing to die rather than accept changes that they did not want.

It was also during that time that he realized that he needed to put in practice some of the theories he had been espousing on urban church renewal. The story of his time as senior pastor in a downtown congregation is well documented in the book *Borderland Churches: A Congregation's Introduction to Missional Living.*[2] It was there that he framed a theological and foundational belief about why the church exists and how it can join in the mission of God. This once proud congregation in the center of the city of Edmonton in Alberta, Canada, had been in decline for years. Its aging congregation, however, had a sense of hope that something was in their future. It was an exciting revitalization. He was challenged to rethink leadership and change. In fact, it was the challenge of the complexity of urban congregations that excited him the most.

The invitation to lead his denomination's international mission organization took him away from that congregation. This was his next significant leadership role, and it proved equally stretching. Denominations and mission organizations were facing challenges that were part of the shifting world around them. Canadian society has moved quite emphatically toward a post-Christendom framework. Institutional religion was increasingly being marginalized. Local churches were asking insightful questions about the existence of denominations and their mission organizations. Frankly, not all their questions were unfair. Denominations and mission organizations have taken loyalty for granted, and this carelessness brought forth evident dissatisfaction.

The next 10 years were an exciting time of moving a traditional mission delivery organization to a mission facilitation organization. It was a painful change, and it required some radical shifts within the organization. It was here that Gary cut his teeth in nurturing change and leading from the bottom up. This organization needed to become a movement if churches and individuals were going to join them. It has been fun for him to observe the significant next steps the organization has been able to continue to take because of the critical shifts that were made at the beginning of the change process.

After 10 years in his role with the mission organization, Gary has stepped into the leadership of Tyndale University College & Seminary situated in one of the most multicultural cities in the world–Toronto, Canada. Tyndale's rich history of over 120 years is rooted in its ability to meet strategic challenges and societal changes head on. At particular times in history, Tyndale had made geographical moves, reimagined itself institutionally, and now was entering a new season of its life and mission. This new season contained within it a challenge of continuing to develop a 10-year-old initiative toward university status and the move to a new campus, which includes the renovation of a large 60-year-old convent and girls' high school. It also included the 21st-century challenge that all universities and seminaries were facing as post-secondary education undergoes dramatic challenges brought about by the cultural and technological shifts of our times.

As we articulate our initial direction for the coming pages, Gary is attending a conference of seminary presidents. The dialogue and conversations are a profound illustration of the dilemma in which most leaders find themselves. The language of the need for change is urgent and passionate. Everyone knows that seminary education is facing profound changes, but the need to tenaciously hold on to long-held assumptions and signposts of success are difficult to give up. The dialogue continues in the hope that all we would have to do is a nip and tuck of minor surgery so the once-proud days of the past can be recovered. The nip-and-tuck cosmetic changes would allow these leaders to continue to function as if the seminary exists for the same reasons that it did in the previous century. Just one example is the mistaken idea that seminaries in the 21st century exist to train clergy and leaders for professional Christian service in Christendom frameworks of the past. Increasingly, the seminary that Gary serves is receiving students whose intent for theological training is for equipping them not for professional Christian ministry, but to be more effective people of faith in the work vocation they have been called to in business and other areas.

Even the most polite interventional questioning of these assumptions (Gary is after all a Canadian) is received with passive acknowledgement. Later, over coffee, colleagues from other institutions sidle up to Gary and acknowledge their appreciation that he asked the "elephant in the room" question: Why do seminaries exist in the 21st century? This is the question all of them were thinking. The public meetings continue, however, with the old language and the unquestioned assumptions fueling the conversation. It is difficult, but if leaders cannot question the shared and untouchable assumptions of the past, how will others do so?

As is hopefully evident from the above overview of each of our backgrounds, we are drawing from real experience. Peter's experience has been predominantly in the marketplace of business and hospitals. Gary comes from the vantage point of congregational life, revitalizing old denominational mission structures, and now as the head of an educational institution. We are writing at a time where our early experiences are now supported by a much better understanding of the theoretical framework that was foundational to our experience.

Disorienting Times

Every futurist or societal guru you read analyzes the current times as a world that has never been seen before. It is a world characterized by unpredictability and global interconnectedness. These two forces alone create a complexity that defies any attempt to place things in neat and tidy categories. It is a world of constant change in which only the nimble and quick responders appear to be able to thrive.

Open a newspaper or log into an online news feed and you are confronted with familiar themes.

- A company, once the market leader, faces decline and insolvency because their "leading-edge" products and services are now deemed obsolete.
- Countries enter political and social revolutions for change and then watch as those liberating people turn into autocratic power-driven regimes similar to the one they had toppled. This, in turn, leads to another cycle of revolution and destruction.
- Innocuous events are amplified through the power of social media into worldwide crises.
- Politicians paralyze their governments in a stalemate of ideologies while the people they were elected to serve wait desperately for solutions.
- The famous leader of one of America's largest megachurches admits that one of his core strategies, once trumpeted as the answer to the decline in the church, was instead a great mistake.
- Great churches in the heart of great cities, once vibrant and alive, are now empty shells barely surviving or, worse, boarded up and derelict.
- Boomers wonder if they can ever retire and millennials wonder why the world they are inheriting has lost hope.

A visit to the former headquarters of Kodak in Rochester, New York, tells it all. This once giant of the photography industry is now an empty shell. An inability to anticipate the seismic shifts taking place in society and adjust quickly to the innovations of digital imaging that they themselves invented rendered them insignificant and irrelevant in just a few decades.

Part of the disorientation comes because shifts happen even more quickly in the 21st century. Canadians are well aware of Blackberry, an icon in the mobile phone market. Blackberry, once the mobile industry's sign of creativity and business standard, is now in free-fall simply because leadership in the bravado of confidence and illusion of their own making failed to read the cues and anticipate the change in time to adjust to the markets around them.

Joshua Cooper Ramo calls these disorienting times "the age of the unthinkable."[3] He points out that nations no longer dominate in the ways they used to and new actors emerge seemingly from nowhere, shaking the world's balance and safety. For instance, a small band of terrorists abduct two hundred girls from a school in Nigeria. World powers posture and even devise well-intended but meaningless Internet statements, but fail to make any dent in launching a rescue. They flaunt the impotence of former methodologies from a much simpler time.

Nothing less than a reinvention of how we view and understand our world is required. We must innovate and constantly anticipate the changes around us. Whether it is a public trading company, a thriving business, or a church seeking to engage the surrounding community in new ways, bringing about a reinvention is all about resilience and a willingness to adapt.

If the rapidity of the shifts and turns of an ever-changing world is not your cup of tea, then this will be an increasingly difficult world for you in which to live. As Ramo writes, "Change in our world isn't going to feel like something far away from us."[4] It is all around us and occurs at the same time as we are adjusting to the previous shifts. It will only get faster and our confusion will become more pronounced, especially if we continue to cling to the old assumption that implementing a strategic plan will lead to stability and no more need for change.

Jean Lipman-Blumen describes the multiple changes taking place in the context that leadership is exercised. Combined with the amplification of rapid technological advances, the ways in which leadership decisions are made has been drastically altered. She states some of the challenges:[5]

- Leaders are confronted with shorter and shorter time frames. Speed and agility are essential.
- Leaders get few second chances. They are pressured to get it right the first time.
- Leaders need new ways of diagnosing and solving labyrinthine problems.
- Leaders have to forge new and innovative solutions because the past solutions no longer work and are irrelevant.
- Leaders need to envision and achieve goals stretching beyond the initial problem–in fact, far beyond their organization's walls and national borders. They need elevation so they can see the big picture.
- Leaders have to think for the long term, despite pressures to succeed in the short term and uncertainties about the future.
- Leaders face unparalleled ethical dilemmas generated by unimagined circumstantial, relational, and technological opportunities. From Wall Street to the White House, Bay Street to Ottawa, constituents have begun to demand new ethical standards in places where ethics were simply stated as just "being honest."

In addition to the list of Lipman-Blumen's leadership challenges, there are several characteristics of these times we wish to highlight.

1. Shifts in the Expectations Placed on Leaders

What we expect and need from leaders is undergoing shifts. In the past, leaders were seen as geniuses with a thousand helpers. They were granted respect, however grudgingly, for the positional authority they held. This is no longer the case. Ethical indiscretions by leaders whose loyalty to the bottom line was more about their bonuses at the end of the year than the health of the organization has eroded trust over the last decades.

As a result, the people who make up the organization's work force tend to function out of a deep sense of distrust for authority. Employees and even church members in voluntary associational relationship have grown to be suspicious of those who choose to lead. This growing erosion of respect and deference to leaders has joined with a pervasive cynicism in which leaders are targets to be criticized and resisted.

James Hunter writes about this suspicion of leadership. He recognized that many in leadership today feel that they are failing the people they lead. He observes, "Many have long ago recognized that the old ways of leading through command-and-control and barking orders are largely ineffective when working with a diverse workplace … the vast majority of whom do not trust power people."[6]

2. *Organizational Inertia*

Another characteristic of these disorienting times is a kind of organizational malaise and inertia. Long-term employees or church members who remember the days of life and vibrancy are overwhelmed by the changes around them, and in their frustration, they resist either passively or aggressively. Good people find themselves simply tired of the change that either appears unannounced or is foisted on them. What is striking, however, is how unreasonable and irrational the responding emotions can be.

This is illustrated wonderfully by Gary's mother. Her commitment to the church she and Gary's dad have attended for over 60 years is complete. While the church stands in striking need of renewal, each change or innovation has been critiqued over the years by those who remember the glory years of the 1960s. These changes are just too much for these elderly saints who remained and soldiered on after so many left this downtown congregation. They have seen leaders come promising a new future and then go after experiment and tentative strategic directions proved faulty. To be sure, the remaining congregants have been less than open to change, but years of being asked to support new initiatives that do not bear fruit takes a toll on your trust. The congregation is just tired of being experimented on; enough is enough. It is no wonder that Gary's mother says, "I know we need to change, but if they could just wait until I am gone, they can then change all they want!"

A clergy friend of Gary's recognizes this kind of resistance in the church that he serves. The church is located in one of the fastest-changing neighborhood communities in the city of Toronto. Once a highly concentrated white, Anglo Saxon community, the area has morphed into one of the most highly multicultural neighborhoods in the city. Surrounding schools send out notices to parents in numerous languages. The area is a mosaic of cultures supported by commerce geared to each culture group. Some of the freshest condiments and spices outside of India can be found in this neighborhood.

The impact on the life of the church has been enormous. The pastor describes the church as a wonderfully diverse place of over 90 ethnic groups that have brought life and vitality to the congregation. It has also brought conflict. He recounts one old-time parishioner's resistance when he complained about the influx of immigrants by saying, "First they stole our city and now they have stolen my church."

3. Filling the Ego Void

Another trend that deeply concerns us is what appears to be a growing personal neediness of some leaders. Self-referential leaders, whose need for success or effectiveness is driven by ego or the need for affirmation, can create chaos for organizations. Clergy leaders increasingly find themselves trapped in this theme. In a society that increasingly marginalizes the church, the minister's role becomes even more irrelevant and misunderstood outside the walls of the church building. The result is the desire to find affirmation in the last places where clergy still hold some place of significance and influence – the institutions of church and denominational life.

The growing marginalization of the occupation of minister and its accompanying sense of social irrelevance were clearly illustrated to Gary a few years ago. Having arrived late to the hospital, he rushed into the waiting area of the operating room where one of the members of his congregation was about to have surgery. Confronted by the head nurse who informed him that he was not allowed to enter, Gary blurted out a plea of significance. "I am here to pray for Jeanne. I promised that I would pray with her before she went into surgery. I am her pastor."

"Where is your hospital badge?" she asked. Sheepishly, he admitted that he had not obtained a badge but would be doing so really soon. She then asked, "Do you have a business card?" Again, with great embarrassment, Gary admitted that he did not have a business card with him. It was then she informed him that he would not be able to enter.

In his need to see Jeanne and to pray with her, Gary pleaded with one last petition. "Look," he said, "being the pastor of First Baptist Church is probably the least relevant and socially significant occupation in this city. Would I tell you I was its pastor if I wasn't?" Gary saw her pause for a moment, and then with a smile and a nod, she allowed him to enter. Gary remembers this with both sadness and relief: relief that he got to pray with Jeanne but sadness that even this head nurse knew the irrelevancy of his profession in a changing society.

We are in a time in which we must ask what happens to the organization when it is being used to fulfill the ego needs of the leader. We also must ask why many leaders are so hollow and empty that they turn to the organization they are leading to fill that void. It is critical to consider the effect on both the leader and the church or organization of this mutual and unhealthy dependency.

Attempting to find affirmation in the jobs we have or the roles we play, relevant or not, is unhealthy. Doing so often leads to an increasing unawareness of ourselves, and this disconnects us from how others perceive us.

Brian Craig is a friend and colleague of Gary's who holds the leadership development portfolio for his denomination.[7] He is often in conversation with pastoral leaders who self-describe as having a particular personality or skill set that, to Brian, does not seem to match the realities of who they really are.

His engagement with these pastoral leaders who are living this disconnect makes him want to ask, "Have you met yourself?" Brian offers this explanation of his startling question:

> The starting point is **self-awareness**. How can I lead based on who I am, if I haven't taken the energy and time to know who I am? If we haven't truly met ourselves, the way we lead will be inauthentic, the worst leadership possible in our day. Tim Keel, in *Intuitive Leadership*, writes, "To give the gift of oneself, of authenticity amid a world consumed by façade, is a necessity and a demonstration of the nature of the God revealed in Jesus Christ. If hypocrisy is the cardinal sin in a postmodern context, then authenticity is the cardinal virtue."[8] Reggie McNeal, in *Practicing Greatness: 7 Disciplines of Extraordinary Spiritual Leaders*, places self-awareness as the first of seven disciplines for effective leading.[9]
>
> So meet yourself. Know how you work. Know how you relate to people. Know the strengths you bring to any situation in which you find yourself. Know what stirs your heart, and as a result, what you can stir in others. Some of "meeting yourself" is about knowing the gaps and struggles, too. But don't let that be the focus. Your greatest leading comes by leaning into your God-given abilities, talents, and aspirations. Meet yourself in the pain of failures so that you meet the strength you've been given to rise beyond that failure. Take up the raw material of your gifts and abilities and lead in that manner. Lead from who you are, not as someone you wish you were or as the person a board or consistory might ask you to be. Meet yourself, and lead that way.

4. *Lacking Certain Skills*

One aspect of the times that make them so disorienting is that everything is up for grabs. Matters of morality, values, and spirituality are a buffet of choices where you can take what you like and leave what does not feel good. Choice has become the order of the day. Having choice is wonderful as long as we have the tools to navigate and negotiate those choices with confidence. The problem is that typical academic preparation has not given us the required leadership skill set of navigating and negotiating.

Today's options are so endless that they almost paralyze us. How do I choose? How do I live with others who have not chosen similarly? Combine this reality with the social norm of tolerance that says that no one has the right to tell anyone else what is right or what to do with their lives, and it is no wonder we feel inert. We are discovering that tolerance is not unending or without intolerance.

We as individuals are plugged into multiple technological devices that demand instant responses, and we suffer from "continuous partial attention." In addition, the pace of life and the multiplicity of options can easily overwhelm people in our culture. Even in conservative, more traditional communities where people have some background in spiritual truth and still have at least a modicum of respect for authority, activities such as children's sports schedules, work demands, and social events can consume a well-meaning person's time and energy.

The Challenges and Possibilities of Disorienting Times

As inalterable changes were taking place in Europe toward the end of the last century, Vaclav Havel wrote: "Something is on the way out and something else is painfully being born. It is as if something were crumbling, decaying and exhausting itself, while something else, still indistinct, were arising from the rubble. … We are in a phase when one age is succeeding another, when everything is possible."[10]

Great possibilities bring great challenges. Peter Senge puts it well:

> Poised at the millennium, we confront two critical challenges: how to address deep problems for which hierarchical leadership alone is insufficient and how to harness the intelligence and spirit of people at all levels of an organization to continually build and share knowledge. Our responses may lead us, ironically, to a future based on more ancient – and more natural – ways of organizing: communities of diverse and effective

leaders who empower their organizations to learn with head, heart, and hand.[11]

We consider Senge's observation incredibly hopeful, for the "ancient" ways of organizing are ways that are aligned with kingdom values. The following are just a few.

Relationships Are Key

The need for a leadership style that is essentially and foundationally relational is critical. The base line for understanding the leadership task in the 21st century is the acknowledgment that we live in an intricately woven systemic dependence on relationships for organizational health. We need one another and the abilities we each bring to face the challenges that emerge. Social and relational intelligence are not only new requirements of the times we are in; they are essential for leadership impact.

For years, Margaret Wheatley has studied leadership in the United States. She observes that people are on a quest to find a new way of working together.[12] The rapidity of change and the isolation caused by problems they cannot solve alone are fertile ground for re-envisioning the organization as community and for taking this idea into the church and actually making it a reality. Leaders become the models of how this can happen. They become the relational trendsetters. We have much more to say about this critical leadership characteristic and will do so in later chapters.

Respect the Context

Leaders function in particular contexts. Ignoring the uniqueness of each context is done at the leaders' peril. Usually these contexts are places in which tradition is so intrinsically part of the organization that leading innovation is significantly different and a much longer process than in start-ups or new church development.

We are often asked if an existing organization can actually change or if change requires completely new structures. The answer is a clear maybe–new structures are not always required, and in fact, most leadership is done in organizations that have context and history. There is no doubt that starting from scratch is faster and allows leaders an opportunity to white board organizational values.

We recognize that educational institutions in general are by nature slow to change and adapt. Outside accrediting bodies bring form and content to much of what needs to take place in the academy, but they are notoriously always in the mode of catching up to the innovation around them. The seminary we serve has been able to innovate curriculum and delivery systems in remarkable ways, allowing the emergence of a new entrepreneurial direction because it is led by skilled leadership. However, the speed at which this innovation can be enacted is stunted by the systems of checks and balances, committees and councils from which decisions must be made. Quick decisions and nimble responses are almost impossible.

One way we moved forward was to place all of the free-standing entrepreneurial centers under one umbrella. It has become an incubator for new ideas. Peter now directs this entity. It is called the Tyndale Open Learning Centre. It is amazing to see which ideas get traction and how quickly responses can be made to declared needs. The potential for innovation and creativity is multiplied when a staff, made up mostly of practitioners, is given the freedom to build from the ground up. Content is given shape. Failure is allowed, and the results have been innovative and energetic.

One branch of the Centre is the Tyndale Intercultural Ministries Centre (TIM Centre). Its intent is to focus on the changing face of a multicultural city. Its programs emerged from a real need within the ethnic communities for ongoing theological learning. Leadership at the TIM Centre, for example, sensed a growing need expressed by diaspora leaders who were beginning new churches in the city. Traditional programs of study were financially inaccessible and not contextually shaped to the needs these leaders were facing. Because of that expressed need, TIM Centre leadership developed a two-year diploma program for pastoral training and missional church leadership in consultation with the leaders of these churches. The results were amazing. Over a hundred graduates have come through the program in the last four years. Recently, over 30 graduates–part of the great migration to Toronto from around the world–celebrated the second graduation from the diploma program. As a result of this and other grassroots initiatives, a trust between intercultural groups throughout the city has been fostered. Larger research universities have contracted with the TIM Centre because they recognize the foundation of trust and care for the community that has developed.

Most of us will not have the luxury or even the opportunity to work from a white board of organizational beginnings. Instead we will find ourselves in organizations and churches desperately in need of change or re-missioning. Leadership will mean leading organizations into a continual process of reinventing themselves so that they will exist in their present dynamically.

The processes of change will take time and require a skill set that enables living in the "not yet" while moving toward the "what can be." New structures will eventually emerge in the existing frames. Quick and radical change only typically emerges when an organization or congregation has come to a place of near death. Still, organizations can find hope.

Particular leaders and styles are best suited for certain situations, but all leaders function within a context in which the role of leadership may be seen and envisioned in very different ways by people within the organization. Gary often says, "Good ministry is good ministry. The only thing that changes is context." We argue the same truth for leadership. Good leadership is good leadership, but it will look profoundly different as it is worked out in different contexts. Leadership in rural Iowa will be profoundly different than in a cosmopolitan urban center such as Toronto.

Transformative Learning

We have already introduced the work of Jack Mezirow. He is a leading thinker in the area of adult learning, and he is the one who refers to "disorienting dilemmas."[13] Writing in the area of transformative learning, a disorienting dilemma occurs when an indicator of the past no longer points toward a predictable direction. These dilemmas are disorienting because the signposts and assumptions that have allowed successful navigation in the past no longer serve us in the ways they did before. In new realities, the old signposts may be the very things that get in our way.

As recently as the summer of 2014, we saw this acted out at Gordon College. A letter signed by the President of Gordon College, along with a number of other leaders of Christian organizations and sent to U.S. President Obama, created an unimagined furor. It was a clear and simple letter, written out of past assumptions, asking for exemption under the auspices of religious freedom from the new labor laws being implemented at that time. This innocent action played out under historical expectations received an unanticipated backlash.

In response to the letter, the *Boston Globe* published an exposé on Gordon's "Community Standards Statement." The town in which Gordon College has been located for decades immediately rescinded long-held rental agreements with Gordon for some of their buildings. Simultaneously, the accrediting body for universities and colleges in the New England area announced a review of Gordon College's accreditation qualifications. The Gordon College community reeled from the avalanche of reactions, stunned by an unanticipated backlash .

Once again, Ramo accurately describes our current situation. He writes, "In a revolutionary era of surprise and innovation, you need to learn to think and act like a revolutionary. People that don't act that way have a particular name: victims."[14] In times of unthinkable and discontinuous change (a change process that never ends), we need to learn to think transformatively by attending to the disorienting dilemmas. In the next chapters, we will lay out the frameworks and the methods in which transformation and change can take place.

Transformative learning requires a very painful first step – unlearning. Unlearning is the intentional questioning of all of our assumptions and models. This requires a mindset that considers nothing as sacred and everything as up for grabs. It's a mindset willing to admit that the assumptions that drove and shaped the organization to this point may indeed be "wanting" in the present and the future.

This understanding is particularly critical for people ful-filling leadership roles in organizations. Their assumptions drive the organizations. Their assumptions inform their decisions and frame their strategic directions. If they do not learn to rethink old assumptions as well as stay alert to the emerging shifts and signs, how will the organization be able to do so?

Unchallenged assumptions are often shaped by sentimentality and deep emotion. Some of those assumptions may not be inherently wrong. They simply do not work anymore. They do not reflect the type of responses necessary for the times we are in. Traditions are important, but over time, if unexamined, their significance and impact are weakened. When organizational leaders sentimentally hold to these deep assumptions without examining their meaning, they lose the ability to ask, "Do they work anymore?" The more blatantly apparent it is that the old assumptions are failing and the more deeply held they are for meaning, the more difficult it may be to question them.

Nevertheless, we are convinced that organizations paddling the white water of disorienting times can change and thrive. At the same time, we are conscious that many are still in the search for the magic program that will enable them to keep doing what they have always done before, just better. We realize how difficult it is to question the old assumptions and signposts of effectiveness, but we do not know any other way that really leads to effective and relevant change.

A Note for the Church

We have a particular concern and a love for the church. We are also her greatest critics. Sometime in our history we lost our moorings around what it means to be the church. It is not the purpose of this book to analyze why this took place. What is more important is to realize that institutionalized and insular views of church life made us unable to engage culture in significant ways. When those cultures and societies began to change, we were impotent to speak into those changes in any meaningful way because we had rendered ourselves irrelevant. Our insularity has been our downfall. Tradition and traditionalism became the entrenchments from which we lived. Tradition is fundamentally different from traditionalism. Jaroslav Pelikan, in *The Vindication of Tradition*, characterized the difference when he wrote, "Tradition is the living faith of the dead; traditionalism is the dead faith of the living....

Traditionalism supposes that nothing should ever be done for the first time ...."[15]

We failed to challenge these institutionalized and insular Christendom foundations and, as a result, entered into a kind of mission-drift that was more about survival and less about our mission and purpose. We spent most of our time focusing on cosmetic alterations of how we packaged church, tailoring ourselves with more contemporary clothes in the desperate hope that people would find us more attractive. Like many public companies that enter the same journey, we found ourselves in the Kodak-like journey toward irrelevance and decline.

We lost our compass direction and settled too often for pale imitations of what really could be. The challenge was to examine our core beliefs about church and our assumptions, but we did not show up for the discussion. And, to be honest, our leaders neither had the courage nor the skills to lead us in that process. As a result, we find ourselves in a time of great shifts. Shifts that bring implications on what leadership will need to be about in the coming years. From a Canadian perspective, we are simply a time-lapse camera as to where the United States is heading. The shifts we have noticed in our context above the 49th parallel include the following:

- **From relative similarity to cultural pluralism.** There was a time where one story gathered and dominated all other stories in Canada. Even though Canada imaged itself as a mosaic of cultures unlike the "melting pot" image in the United States, this multicultural diverse affirmation was still taking place with one dominant voice and influence. This is no longer so. For example, we live in a city, Toronto, where over 49.9 percent of the population is foreign-born. Toronto has become a multicultural reality where the world has come to its neighborhoods. Younger generations are no longer surprised or intimidated by this new situation. What impact does this change have on how we do business? What does church look like in a multicultural context?
- **From church at the core to a decentered church**. European cities are built around town squares that

often have at their heart a church or cathedral. One only has to travel for a short time in Europe to be reminded how de-centered the church really has become in after-Christendom Europe. Too often, the churches in the squares are museums or concert halls and, if they are home to a worshipping community, their buildings come alive only a few times a week. This is a social reality for the Canadian church. In fact, it is really a question about whether religion and the church even have a place at the table.

• **From church as familiar to church as a new social reality.** In the Canadian context, more and more Canadians have less and less Christian memory. We live in an after-Christendom world that is quickly becoming a new reality in the United States as well. In a way, this shift has become a healthy one as it has witnessed the decline of religious nominalism. Timothy Tennant from Asbury Theological Seminary makes the point that one of the downsides of Christendom was that it fostered religious nominalism–church attendance as a cultural norm but not a life-shaping force in one's life. As Christendom has declined in Canada, there has been a clear sorting out; less and less people go to church, but more and more know why they are going. This new social reality has put the church in unfamiliar territory, leaving many within the church feeling uncomfortable. We do not know who we are, and those outside the church are not sure who we are either. The implications of this shift are enormous. Within our churches, changes must take place at deeper levels than the cosmetic changes we too often make trying to shape the church to appear more like everything else people's experience.

We must realize we have lost our way. Our reason for existence in the first place is nearly forgotten. Like a department store chain that after years of tinkering with shelving, lighting, and new product in the attempt to stem the tide of decline, finally asks the question "why?" and not just "how" and "what."

For the church, it means asking why God formed the church in the first place and for what purpose. The implications that emerge from the answers to these questions are enormous. Leaders of the church caught in the models of success placed before them are trapped. If they do not examine these models in the light of theological and biblical views of the church, they will become victims of every wind of a new idea and fad. Models are only helpful if rooted in a deep abiding sense of why the church or organization exists in the first place. We believe that place is found in the mission of God and in his passionate purposefulness.

Another Book on Leadership

This book is about leadership in disorienting times. We are writing this book with the deep commitment that this is actually a great time to be in leadership and a great time to be in the church. The fact that everything is up for grabs is something we find exciting. The fact that leadership has become a courageous act in the swirl of constant change means to us that the day belongs to the nimble and the adaptive. We invite each of us to contain our ego-centeredness so that change and creativity can emerge from within and so that leadership can be a shared process. Change is a collective action orchestrated by confident and grounded leaders who believe that more than one individual can influence its process of change.

Almost every leadership book quotes Peter Senge and we are no exception. He writes: "We are coming to believe that leaders are those people who 'walk ahead,' people who are genuinely committed to deep change in themselves and in their organizations. They lead through developing new skills, capabilities, and understandings. And they come from many places within the organization."[16]

Leadership in the 21st century requires a social and relational IQ that stimulates collective action and engenders trust. We want to suggest that disorienting times require disorienting leaders. Focusing on change within any organization–whether it be a congregation, denomination, business, or hospital–we explore the principles that are embodied in leaders so passionate about what they hope to see happen in the world around them that they are willing to lead differently, confidently, and from the bottom up.

2

From Kirk to Picard

*They are somewhat self-effacing individuals who deflect
adulation, yet who have an almost stoic resolve to do
absolutely whatever it takes to make the company great,
channeling their ego needs away from themselves and into the
larger goal of building a great company.*
–Jim Collins, "The Misguided Mix-up of
Celebrity and Leadership"

*I will take the Ring to Mordor ... though I do not know the
way.*
–Frodo, The Fellowship of the Ring

Peter has hiring teams of public, private, and social sector
organizations consulting with him about what they want and
need in a leader. Gary serves denominations, seminaries, and
universities in similar ways. These hiring teams talk about the
qualities of the leader needed to enable them to navigate through
the confusing times in which they find themselves. However, the
language these teams use is profoundly dissonant with the type
of leadership to which they would respond. It is as though they
want the retired highly successful American business executive
and author Jack Welch in the younger, sleeker body of Malcolm
Gladwell–Canadian journalist, bestselling author, and speaker.
The truth is that leadership has changed, and the Messiah-like

person for whom the hiring teams are searching does not exist. Our friend Leonard Hjalmarson makes the point this way:

> Instead of the Lone Ranger, we have Frodo–the Clint Eastwoods and Sylvester Stallones are replaced by ordinary men. Frodo, Aragorn and Neo (the Matrix) are self-questioning types who rely on those around them for strength, clarity and purpose. Indeed, while they have a sense of the need and a willingness to sacrifice themselves, they may not even know the first step on the journey. This is a far cry from the self-assured presentation of the John Maxwells and Rick Warrens of the world. It is equally distant from the Greek heroic journey. Indeed, the contrast we are seeing is sharper the further we travel along the road from modernity to post-modernity.[1]

Many authors in the leadership field have commented on the change of preferred leadership style by comparing it to the change in leaders in the Star Trek series from Captain Kirk to Jean Luc Picard. Kirk is the quintessential confident Alpha male CEO. Power is concentrated in his "seat" as he barks orders to all. The organization looks to him because he has the plan. Power and authority are granted by his position and role, and it is that role that gives him the right to lead. And lead he does. He shouts commands, and he pushes himself forward so he can lead his ship *the Enterprise* into the fray.

Picard, on the other hand, leads by listening, embodying the deep commitment that he and his team together can solve problems. His leadership is positioned almost like that of a fellow traveler on the journey. Power and authority are distributed and interconnected. Relationships are critical to the efficient and effective solving of the presenting episodic issue; trust and relationship give the right to lead.

One other characteristic that emerges out of both Star Trek series is the fact that leaders exude confidence in themselves and the others around them. This is illustrated well in an episode of *Star Trek: The Next Generation* when Captain Picard and the ship's doctor are stranded alone on some imaginary planet and their brains are linked by some kind of alien device, allowing them to read each other's thoughts. The captain declares, "We're going this way." The doctor replies quickly with great disdain, "You don't know which way to go, do you?" She can read his thoughts.

Captain Picard explains to her that sometimes being a leader means just picking a way and being confident about it because people want to be led. There are times when you just have to lead, even if you do not have all the answers. Captain Picard would affirm that leaders may not have all the answers and, as is evident in the above scenario, a leader ought to even admit it. The blind side of having all the answers is not listening to others. Perhaps good leadership means being willing to have the confidence to move forward even when all the answers needed are not yet available.

A number of years ago, Warren Bennis noted similar emerging changes in leadership. He said, "We need to move to an era in which leadership is an organizational capability and not an individual characteristic that a few individuals at the top of the organization have."[2] Steve Bornstein and Anthony Smith make a similar comment: "Leadership is now understood by many to imply collective action orchestrated in such a way as to bring about significant change while raising the competencies and motivation of all those involved."[3]

Joseph Rost, after a detailed analysis of leadership literature in the 20th century, posits that leadership in our current context is "an influence relationship among leaders and followers who intend real changes that reflect their mutual purposes."[4] Again, the emphasis is on the inherently relational, not authoritative, nature of leadership.

"You can do that, you are the President!" Gary heard this declaration countless times in his first years as President at Tyndale. It is a remarkable statement of the power of positional authority, one that may be said of a leader like Captain Kirk. The context of the comment is often when consensus has been difficult to reach. Other times, it comes when compromise that might lead to consensus is being withheld. To many, it appears that his office gives him unlimited power to make decisions in a way that no one else can. The president is able to dictate from above with seemingly unlimited authority.

At one level, there is a measure of safety for the member of the organization who does not make or who does not enter into the making of decisions. If the member of the organization relinquishes or outright defers the responsibility of participating in the decision making, it allows that person to stay at arm's length of the decision. If anything goes wrong, members like this are able to quickly remove themselves from the decision because they never owned it in the first place. Of course, they live with the consequences of the decisions made, but they can do so from a distance and with a condescending stance. They can critique the one or ones who did step up and enter in the decision. This is the downside of the office. It can be lonely at the top if the members play the distancing game and, even more so, if the leader chooses to play along by living and leading from there.

Gary has come to learn that his preferred style of leadership is more of the Captain Picard type than that of Captain Kirk. He is a consensus builder. It is not that he is unable to be decisive, though he confesses that at times it may appear that he is slower than some to come to a decision. He is even willing to take full responsibility for the decision made if it goes wrong. He prefers, however, the ownership that comes from taking the time to bring people into the decision-making process. It leads to more enlightened and informed decisions. It also creates more passionate participation. So he has grown to prefer this consensus-building style. It is what we are coming to understand as servant leadership.

Can Servanthood and Leadership Go Together?

We suggest that the leadership style of Captain Picard is akin to what we have come to describe as the servant leader. The servant leader is certainly not the independent maverick who walks to the "beat of a different drum." Nor is the servant leader the rugged individual who is typically worshipped in movies and celebrated in magazines. The authoritarian, autocratic leader Jack Welch is not the first executive to adopt a style that conflicts with the notion of servant leadership. Servanthood is not an idea many people associate with leadership. Even Jim Collins in his book *Good to Great* struggled with the word "servant." The best he could come up with was "Type 5" leaders. He comments: "The mistaken belief held by many directors is that a high-profile, larger-than-life leader is required to make a company great. As a consequence companies and congregations keep putting people into positions of power who lack the inclination to become Level 5 leaders [Collin's phrase for servant leader]. The result is predictable, more of the same."[5]

Why is there such confusion and reticence for the word "servant?" Maybe it conjures up a sense of being "servile" and, in our times of self-actual individualization, this idea is anything but appealing. We fear the idea of denigrating ourselves. Instead our society has embraced the idea of self-esteem, self-honor. While serving may in fact be a more honoring approach to leadership, our society may be too self referential to be able to value the other, which is an aspect of servanthood.

Still, after extensive study, Collins and many others conclude that healthy and effective organizations have servant leaders. They may find the word *servant* difficult to use, but they cannot escape the fact that something different and better takes place when servant leadership is exercised.

Robert Greenleaf introduced the term *servant* into current leadership literature many years ago.[6] He stated:

> The servant-leader is servant first. It begins with the natural feeling that one wants to serve. Then conscious choice brings one to aspire to lead. The best test is: do those served grow as persons: do they, while being served, become healthier, wiser, freer, more autonomous, more likely themselves to become servants? And, what is the effect on the least privileged in society; will they benefit, or, at least, not be further deprived?[7]

Secular management and leadership consultants increasingly reflect deeply on this idea of leadership from a servant perspective. Simon Sinek, the writer and management speaker heralded for his book on the why of business, recently explored this theme in a book entitled *Leaders Eat Last*.[8] In the foreword to the book, George J. Flynn, Lieutenant General of the Marine

Corps, wrote, "A leader who takes care of their people and stays focused on the well-being of the organization can never fail."

Regardless of their faith affiliations, Sinek, Flynn, and others are simply articulating the same servanthood that is meant to be the revolutionary framework of Christianity. Embodied in Jesus who came "not to be served but to serve," it stands as the radical center of the Christian life. Unfortunately, this has gotten lost in the Christian community's discussion on leadership where servanthood is too often intermingled with the role of pastoral caregiving and a chaplaincy model of the pastoral role. This limited image fails to grasp the courageous and intentional nature of a servant leadership that is grounded in the God who models in Jesus a proactive, courageous, and intentional servanthood. As result, we appear to have declared our preference for Captain Kirk's leadership style–leaning on the charismatic bigger-than-life leader who disdains or only plays lip service to the concept of servanthood as the foundational base from which leadership emerges.

Servant leaders do not act from a passive position. Servant leaders do not simply wait to be told what to do. Their call to vocation generally and leadership particularly has within it a deep sense of purpose, living a call which is characterized by urgency and courage. Servant leaders have dreams, and they have the ability to portray this vision in vivid language. They do not just wait patiently for others to come up with the idea. If anything is going to happen, they realize that there must be a dream or a grand purpose to which all are called to be dream weavers. The greatest leaders are those who can describe the dream or grand purpose in such a way that it becomes crystal clear to the listeners and motivates them to join in its creation.

Gary is part of a denomination that has, unfortunately, made this "passive" leadership style an art form. He calls it the non-leadership leadership style. Years of denominational infighting, personality conflicts, and theological controversy formed a people so afraid of conflict that, as one denominational leader stated, "We have begun to believe that our role is to make sure that leaders don't get away with anything and, because big vision is destructive, we make sure it never gets implemented." While this passive leadership style works itself out differently in each region of Canada, it contains within its DNA the practice of isolating strong servant leaders. Ironically, this denomination's life and ethos actually produces remarkable leaders, but they just do not know what to do with them. The result has been the nurturing of a view of pastoral and lay leadership that ultimately is blown to and fro by the winds of self-interest or personal preference so often encapsulated in a faulty view of congregational governance.

During times of conflict, these traits are intensified by pastoral leaders who simply want to passively please and care for people. William Willimon humorously overstates that tendency for people entering the ministry to want to help people. He says this motivation to help others is dangerous because you can never do enough. As he states, "If you are motivated to go into the pastoral ministry because you 'want to help people,' you will die. It will be like being nibbled to death by a duck."[9] This style, however, is so embedded in the psyche and DNA of this particular denomination that those courageous enough to desire to lead differently are often marginalized. One particular leader, for example, is a sought-after speaker in conferences around North America, but he is often ridiculed and diminished within his own denominational life.

Robert Greenleaf made similar observations as he entered into dialogue with church leaders. He began to realize that they described servant leadership in very passive and maintenance-like frameworks. He observed church leaders who often used the concept of servanthood as the reason they do not act proactively. In truth, he discovered, it is simply because these leaders were unsure of their role and therefore unable to lead intentionally or proactively. It was quite telling that during the early 1970s when Greenleaf was writing, he was largely ignored by the church.

Theological training has tended to reinforce this idea of clergy as chaplain and prime caregiver of the congregation. Seminaries have focused on a pastoral care model that has emphasized a chaplaincy framework in which the primary role was to serve the congregation in an "I'll meet your needs at all costs" framework. Leadership was downplayed as we worshipped at the altar of the priestly role of ministry where we became purveyors of care and grace. We failed, however, to hold that role in tension with the prophetic role of ministry leadership that calls people to a costly discipleship. Without this tension between the priestly and prophetic role, servant leadership is void of courage and edge. There is no doubt in our minds that it was the deference to a passive pastoral care view of servant leadership that served as a contributing factor to the decline and growing irrelevance of the church in an increasingly secular world.

The commitment to servanthood can at times be a courageous and intentional choice. For example, it was not a timid, weak, or servile spirit that caused Jesus to describe the Pharisees as a "brood of vipers" (Matt. 3:7; 12:34; 23:33). Jesus had all the power and authority of heaven, but, as Paul writes in Philippians 2:7, "He emptied himself, taking the form of a slave." This is the paradox of servant leadership: it is both a choice and a non-negotiable call of the one to whom we play our lives.

The Servant Leader

For the Christian, the model of the servant leader is Jesus himself. Low prestige, low respect, and low honor were part of Jesus' embodiment of servant. More so, his definitions of key concepts in leadership were strangely different from those that were common in his time and in ours. He turned ideas of greatness, power, and authority upside down. It is no wonder that he was so unsettling.

His confrontation of James and John in Mark 10 is a striking example. Theirs was a simple request: "Let us sit at your right and left hand when you rule." Jesus' response turned their thinking. The disciples had been conditioned to think about leadership as hierarchical, rooted in power and authority. Jesus' paradigm is based on servanthood, and he names it. "You know," he says, "that among the Gentiles those whom they recognize as their rulers, lord it over them, and their great ones are tyrants over them" (Mark 10:42). In this social commentary, there is biting irony in the reference to those who give the illusion of ruling but simply exploit the people over whom they exercise dominion. These leaders struggle for rank and precedence. Their desire to exercise authority is for their own advantage. The tragedy of this story in Mark's gospel is that the disciples were actually imitating those whom they undoubtedly despised.

Jesus strikes a contrast between this top-down framework that is their experience and the way of the kingdom that he is about. He interrupts their misunderstanding with a declaration of the Good News of the Kingdom that introduces a new order where authentic community and communion are constituted and maintained through the servanthood of leadership.

"Not so with you," Jesus declares with uncharacteristic bluntness (v. 43). These are not words of suggestion; nor is he offering this option as one among many. These are declarative words, stating with stark clarity that "this is how it is." From Jesus' perspective, leadership is first and foremost about being a servant (*diakonos*), and ultimate power is about ultimate submission, as a slave (*doulos*): "whoever wishes to become great among you must be your servant, and whoever wishes to be first among you must be slave of all. For the Son of Man came not to be served but to serve, and to give his life a ransom for many" (vv. 43–44).

Matthew tells a similar story and frames it around the question, "Who is the greatest in the kingdom of heaven?"(Matt. 18:1). This was a pressing question for the disciples in their desperate search for position and prestige. Jesus responds by calling a little child to come forward. It is then he makes a revolutionary statement. "Whoever becomes humble like this child is the greatest in the kingdom of heaven" (v. 4). Too often this passage is preached or taught focusing on the idea of the innocence of childlikeness. Jesus' statement was not about innocence. It was about humility and dependency.

Jesus' new reality was obviously difficult to grasp. A few chapters later, these disciples attempt to get rid of the children who have come to see Jesus, and it again becomes a teaching moment (Matt. 19:13–14). The disciples are embarrassed that once again they have missed the point. These children are the kind of people for whom his kingdom is established, he reminds them. Power, prestige, and even authority are very different to Jesus, and he wants to make sure the disciples understand.

To be fair, Jesus was not the kind of Messiah the disciples had expected. He was not the type of King they had been waiting for. It took time and reflection for them to restructure their thoughts and actions. In fact, servant leadership is always a counterintuitive act that requires constant care and nurture.

In Luke 18:9–14, Jesus tells the parable of a Pharisee and a tax collector. These were people whom the disciples knew all too well, and Jesus' story is a challenge to the worldview they held about authority and power. "For all those who exalt themselves will be humbled, and those who humble themselves will be exalted," (v.14, TNIV) he tells them. To the disciples, this was simply a restating of what they had seen at work in their daily life with Jesus: He was constantly challenging the norms and upsetting the structures of their society. He befriended tax collectors, hung out with the marginal, and reprimanded Pharisees; he constantly did the opposite of what was expected. Lest they miss the point, Jesus wanted them to know that these were not isolated events: This was how God's new reign worked and what the Good News of the Kingdom was all about.

To confirm the point, Jesus points ahead to the cross, although it is doubtful anyone understood that at the time. He says, "Even the Son of Man did not come to be served, but to serve, and to give his life as a ransom for many" (Mk. 10:45, TNIV). The use of the word *doulos* is unique in the New Testament, and with it Jesus suggests that the true leader must be willing to forego all sense of identity, all sense of personhood, in service of others.

Robert Munger was a professor of ministry who taught Gary at Fuller Seminary. His ministry had been rich and full both at First Presbyterian Church Berkeley and University Presbyterian Church in Seattle. In the latter part of his life he had come to Fuller to pour himself into the lives of future leaders for the church. His was a gentle style, pastorally rich in its insights but with a sense of strength and commitment.

One day he drew two equilateral triangles on a white board. One had the tip of a 60-degree angle of the triangle pointing up as the triangle sat on its base. The other triangle's 60-degree tip was pointing down, hanging from its base. Above the first triangle he wrote **KING** and **QUEEN**. Below the latter he wrote **SERVANT**.

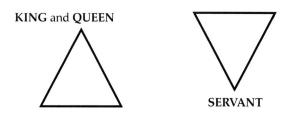

KING and **QUEEN**

SERVANT

The first triangle represents the cultural drive of our times. It represents a leadership actively moving in an effort to get to the top. "Not so," he said, for those who follow Jesus. "Our action is toward the bottom, seeking to serve in such a way that lives and societies are transformed." This is the upside down reign of Christ. This is the radical center and revolutionary act of the followers of Jesus who seek to serve rather than be served. These are the people who believe that the "first shall be last" and to find life you must "lose it."

The apostle Paul describes servanthood in the letter to the Philippians. Having described how the followers of Christ should live with each other, he points to Jesus as the model for what servanthood is all about. He tells us that Jesus, "though he was in the form of God, did not regard equality with God as something to be exploited, but emptied himself, taking the form of a slave [*diakonos*]" (Phil. 2:6–7). This is the paradox of servant leadership. While it is a decision that comes from a deep sense of self, it is not a decision to simply serve but to be a servant. Richard Foster observes that there is a vast difference "between choosing to serve and choosing to be a servant. When we choose to serve, we are still in charge. … But when we choose to be a servant, we give up the right to be in charge."[10]

Jesus' teachings were scandalous to those in power in his day. Not only was he challenging the assumptions of power and authority on which they had built their identities and their possessions, but he was publicly confronting their power-oriented legalistic and socio-economic systems.

Let's be honest. For the most part, we do not get it any

better than the disciples did. What Jesus demonstrated and taught was, and is still, so counter-cultural that just as we think we have grasped it, it escapes us yet again. At times we live in this not-yet experience and it makes us anxious, so we move to exercise control again to get things back in our preconceived box and alleviate our anxiety.

To live as servant leaders is to be in a constant state of reflection as we navigate and negotiate our worlds as leaders. Leaders who live in this state live with an increasing dependence on God and with a high level of accountability to others.

Henri Nouwen wrote, "It is not a leadership of power and control, but a leadership of powerlessness and humility in which the suffering servant of God, Jesus Christ, is made manifest."[11] Nouwen calls us away from a desire for relevance and into a life of prayerful submission to the will of God: "I am deeply convinced that the Christian leader of the future is called to be completely irrelevant and to stand in this world with nothing to offer but his or her own vulnerable self."[12] This self-giving love is captured in the love that God gives us, not because of anything we have done, but simply because of who we are, His creation. Our challenge is to mirror that love back out into the world through acts of service and sacrifice and even in our leadership.

Nouwen's understanding fights every tendency of the human heart to work toward meaning and purpose in life. Instead, meaning and purpose are discovered in the living out of a servant life. Nouwen points out in his book *In the Name of Jesus* that even the temptations of Jesus in the desert are centered on the lure of being relevant – turn stone to bread (be the great provider), tempt death (be superhuman), have all power and dominion (be in complete control). Clearly, Nouwen argues, if Jesus calls us to turn away from the temptation to relevance and into a life of service, the Christ-follower has no choice. Dallas Willard develops even further this challenge of choosing to live a life of service, observing that we neither equip nor affirm its relevance to the Christian life. Nor do we acknowledge in practice its counterpoint reality to the value system so prevalent in the world. He writes:

The discipline of service is even more important for Christians who find themselves in positions of influence, power and leadership. To live as a servant while fulfilling socially important roles is one of the greatest roles any disciple ever faces. It is made all the harder because the church does not give special training to persons engaged in these roles and foolishly follows the world by regarding such people as "having made it," possibly even considering them qualified to speak as authorities in the spiritual life because of their success in the world. [13]

How Do Servant Leaders Lead?

Servant Leaders Know Their Audience of Significance

A Christian perspective on servant leadership acknowledges first and foremost a total devotion to God. It seems like such a cliché, but, increasingly, we are wondering if Christian leaders really do get it. It takes a leader to grow a leader, but inevitably a good leader must first be a follower. Followers know who their audience of significance is and seek to play their lives to the approval and delight of that audience.

Gary first heard this idea of identifying your "audience of significance" from John Claypool, a well-known writer who was the featured speaker at a conference held long ago. Claypool described an insight he had discovered about human nature by observing his own reaction to reviews of his work. He was fascinated that negative reviews did not bother him at all if they came from people whose reactions he did not care about. At the same time, he realized that there were certain people whose evaluations held amazing power. Their words of approval warmed him. Their criticism cut deeply. From these observations he concluded that each one of us has a select audience before whom we play the drama of our lives. It may be one person or a group of persons, but what this person or group thinks exerts enormous influence over our daily actions. In fact, we entrust god-like power to those we choose to be our audience of significance.

Woody Allen's movie *Zelig* is a great illustration of this. The main character, Leonard, fits well into every circumstance because he actually changes his personality to each evolving situation. He rides in a ticker-tape parade with General MacArthur, stands between U.S. President Herbert Hoover and Calvin Coolidge, clowns with prizefighter Jack Dempsey, and discusses theater with playwright Eugene O'Neil. Leonard has no personality of his own, so he assumes whichever strong personality he meets. With the Chinese, he is straight out of China. With rabbis, he miraculously grows a beard and side curls. With psychiatrists, he apes their jargon and strokes his chin with solemn wisdom. At the Vatican, he is part of the Pope's entourage. At spring training, he stands on deck next to Babe Ruth in a Yankee uniform. He is a chameleon changing color, accent, and shape as the world about him changes. He has no ideas or opinions of his own but simply conforms as he plays to the audience of significance around him. He wants to be safe, to fit in, to be accepted, to be liked.

Each one of us has an audience of significance to which we play our lives. Deciding who the audience will be is critical, because it will be the approval of that audience that will matter most to us. It will be the values and priorities of the audience of choice that will emerge. From the perspective of leadership, the decision as to which audience you will choose is a key question to be answered by a leader.

Leaders who play their lives to human audiences are often consumed by whether or not they will be liked by those they lead. They become inconsistent and unpredictable, tossed back and forth by the affirmation of the crowd.

Leadership from a Christian perspective emerges from the acknowledgement that our audience of significance is God. It begins and ends with the belief that God, who in Jesus makes all things possible, creates a place of rootedness and security from which the radical nature of servanthood is possible. Leaders who work out of a place where all the aspects of their lives are touched by what He calls us to be and do, lead more freely and share more openly because their identity is assured.

Isaiah 43 speaks deeply to this rootedness in God. Into the dismal condition of the people of Israel exiled in Babylon, God interrupts their despair. The new world in which they found themselves was crushing them. It was stealing away all aspects of the identity they had had before. The rhythms, occupational roles, and positions in society had been swept away. Once landowners and merchants, they now were servants, slaves, and immigrants. God's passionate response through the writer of Isaiah is a purposeful cry and reminder of who they are in Him.

Isaiah evokes words of call and vocation. He describes the longing of God and what God hopes in his action of bringing us back into relationship. "But now, this is what the LORD says– he who created you, Jacob, he who formed you, Israel: "Do not fear, for I have redeemed you. I have summoned you by name; you are mine" (Isa. 43:1, TNIV). These are words of love and intent. They ring like a bell, calling us to play our lives to something and someone that matters. This is the core identity for the follower of Jesus, and the single purpose for those who lead as God's servants. Be grounded in God and be like Him!

No one in recent history reflected more deeply on this truth than the late Dallas Willard. His work on the interior life of the disciple has been revolutionary in the way that it calls us back to a grounded discipleship. He says:

> As Jesus' disciple, I am his apprentice in kingdom living. I am learning from him how to lead my life in the Kingdom of the Heavens as he would lead my life if he were I. It is my faith in him that led me to become his disciple. My confidence in him simply means that I believe that he is right about everything: all that he is and says shows what life is at its best, what it was intended by God to be. "In him was life and the life was the light of men." (John 1:4 NASB)[14]

Christian institutions and organizations are most effective when they are grounded on this reality. When youth ministries, congregational life, and seminaries root their identity in being the beloved of God, they produce passionate followers of Jesus Christ who form relevant leaders who will be prepared to form the kind of gospel people require for the church of the 21st century. These leaders nurture the formational development of people who do not simply believe in Jesus but believe the things that Jesus believes in and seek to live out those beliefs in the light of all that they implicate.

Disciples are those who, seriously intending to become like Jesus from the inside out, systematically and progressively rearrange their affairs to that end, under the guidance of the Word and the Spirit. That is how disciples live. They are aware and acknowledge that they must work interdependently with others and often in submission to others.

Christian leaders ground their confidence in God's willing–ness and ability to provide the required resources. They take faith-based risks, confident that they lack nothing from God. Their confidence is conformed to the will of God rooted in the journey and the discovery that it is good and perfect.

Paul challenges us to this end in Romans 12. Reflecting on the journey of transformation, he calls us to "present yourselves as living sacrifices to God" and be transformed. He writes, "Do not be conformed to this world, but be transformed by the renewing of your minds, so that you may discern what is the will of God–what is good and acceptable and perfect" (12:2). We become different people as we live in service to God, and therefore we become different leaders.

Leaders who ground themselves on positional or personal power demand that followers conform to their desires and expectations. In contrast, leaders grounded in the "belovedness" of God are able to live with a deeper sense of humility. This humble sensibility acknowledges that the solutions to the challenges they are facing are not simply theirs to solve. They realize that the solution resides in the community of people who make up the organization.

Servant Leaders Lead with Vision

Many clergy and company leaders find the idea of vision-casting leadership particularly appealing in this day and age. While the nurturing pastor had been the predominant image for many in previous generations, the last decades have witnessed the emergence of a desire to lead a congregation through deep change into the promised land of new ministry. It is a coveted image captured in many pastoral conversations. We long to be leaders who serve as visionary catalysts, stimulating the prophetic imagination of a congregation into increased ministry development and growth.

This is no different in the places that Peter has worked. Leaders outside of the church relish the idea of visionary leadership and find it supportive of their desire to cast vision and gain ownership for that vision. All the leadership resources we cite in this book espouse the view that effective leaders articulate compelling visions about the purposes of their organizations and capture the imagination of the people they are called to lead. We would affirm that as a key activity of effective servant leaders.

Visionary leaders assist others to understand what they should be involved with and why it is important. They inspire people to accept responsibility for the implementation of the vision and resource them as they develop a measurement of excellence. Their effectiveness is accomplished because they recognize the limits and realities of their organization. As a result, they define their goals for excellence within those limits. They articulate a vision that empowers people by helping them understand how their efforts contribute to the vision.

James Macgregor Burns calls these people transforming leaders.[15] He realizes that leadership not only makes a difference in the organization but also elicits growth and maturity in the people they are leading. He believes that leadership should raise the vision, beliefs, and aspirations of followers to a new level. Leaders will also shape new sets of values. They do so by articulating, reinforcing, and renewing the values of the organization because of their deep desire to see its members mature and grow.

Servant leadership transforms people to become more than they are today. It encourages value formation, meaning, and even passion to the task. In all they do, effective leaders attempt to deeply embed the values and profound beliefs in the life and rhythm of the congregation so that behaviors of the members reflect the values they articulate. The leadership desire is for transformation and renewal.

Peter has some deep concerns about the way leaders engage in the notion of vision casting. He notes that vision is too often framed in the language of growth and expansion, treating vision more as a destination point than as a process of getting there. That is why in his consulting practice he challenges leaders to reframe vision in terms of purpose where key questions set out a destination as well as the journey to get there. He uses key questions such as: What sort of community do we want to be? What would we experience if we were consistently living out of our defined purpose in a way that reflected our values? Answers to such questions result in a vision that is much more sustainable in highly volatile times where change is taking place constantly.

Gary has been leading Tyndale University College in this very exercise. It has been shaped around the reality that, in the initial stages of their move to undergraduate university status, numerous competing visions have been at work within faculty, staff, students, the board, and the school's constituency. Rather than focusing on what programs needed to be developed, the overarching question has been framed around what kind of university we want to be. Out of that question has emerged the steps in the journey that would lead the university to fulfill that vision–a vision framed experientially rather than structurally or programmatically.

Servant Leaders Fuel Passion

The idea of servant leadership as a modern-day business construct was born out of Greenleaf's pragmatic fascination with how things get done in organizations. After years of working with both small and large organizations, churches, and educational institutions, we have come to realize that very little significant or sustained impact can be accomplished when leaders resort to traditional, autocratic, and hierarchical modes of leadership. While that may have worked at some point on the factory floor, it tends to produce mediocre results when engaging with knowledge workers.

Servant leaders have the capacity to elicit the discretionary energy of those they are called to lead. It is this energy that leads to improved creativity and innovation – a deeper commitment to customers, a willingness to go the extra mile and, ultimately, own the change process itself. It comes from a feeling of being liberated and valued, not from a place of distrust and being supervised. It cannot be coerced or manipulated out of people for very long. It can, however, be nurtured and drawn out by leaders who put a primacy on the unique capacity and potential of each individual who makes up the organization

One of the hospitals with which Peter regularly consults has fully embraced a commitment to distributed leadership framed by a commitment to service. When he looks at clients who have been successful in embracing and leveraging change, he finds dozens of micro-innovations happening every day as people work together to live out daily the core purpose of the organization.

Organizations large and small face overwhelming challenges trying to navigate the permanent white water of disorienting times. The more complex the system, the greater the need for the organization to self-organize out of a deep well of passion and commitment at all levels of the organization.[16] Then and only then can true change happen. If the commitment and passion are not there within the organization, no strategy will work. If systems are restrictive and binding, no amount of change management will be able to facilitate new possibilities.

Servant Leaders Give Permission

The challenge in most organizations is to nurture both a culture and an attitude that recognizes change will be an ongoing reality. By acknowledging that reality, people in the organization have permission to always be asking if is there a better way and to find their own ways of improving the mission and purpose of the organization. Servant leadership provides the fertile ground for this kind of change to occur on a consistent basis.

This was clearly commented on by a hospital CEO in a discussion he was having with a group of emerging leaders. "We will never unlock the key to improved patient satisfaction (a critical performance measure in healthcare) from the executive offices," he said. "We will only do so through you and through serving your needs as the leaders who have real, daily contact with the patients."

It comes from the attitude and commitment that leadership is not solely the purview of the CEO and Senior Team. This attitude must permeate all levels of the organization. It suggests that there is no single way to lead and no single personality that reflects good leadership. It acknowledges that the one underlying theme that binds all members of the organization together is service. In Peter's view, the best way to create change is to work with the particular capabilities that each person has in the organization, while constantly working to improve and expand those capabilities. This approach calls leaders to create change by nurturing an environment in which others are empowered to act on a passionately held focus of the organization's mission, values, and vision.

It is not about a single, all-knowing leader or a hierarchy of manager-leaders. Instead it is a process of influencing the whole organization to centrally focus on the organization's mission, values, and vision. This defines a group's shared purposes and the individual responsibilities each member of the group has to achieve those purposes. It is no wonder that Max De Pree says:

> The goal of thinking hard about leadership is not to produce great or charismatic or well-known leaders. The measure of leadership is not the quality of the head, but the tone of the body. The signs of outstanding leadership appear primarily among the followers. Are the followers reaching their potential? Are they learning? Serving? Do they achieve the required results? Do they change with grace? Manage conflict?[17]

Greenleaf's core definition of leaders as servants suggests that the best test of the leader is simply focused on the results of those they lead. Do those served grow as persons? Leaders are found wooing, coaxing, and even at times prodding people in the relative missional direction in which they believe they are called to go. Leaders are no longer solely found at the head of a pack wanting others to follow them anywhere with unequivocal loyalty. Instead, as Alan Roxburgh writes, "The key to innovating new life and mission in a congregation is not so much a strategy for growth as it is cultivation of people themselves."[18]

Leadership is about nurturing atmospheres, conditions, and attitudes. Leaders serve as stimulators, nurturing a community of fellow travelers seeking to fulfill the mission for which the organization exists. Effective leaders cultivate an atmosphere of encouragement and nurture attitudes within the congregation that promote a missional imagination in congregations or mission-driven commitment in organizations. People are freed to dream and be part of the mission, not simply for its growth but for the organizational development of its structures.

Servant leaders know that people within their churches or organizations come in an array of categories and levels of emotional stability. These leaders desire to encourage greater maturity in all while nurturing the atmosphere that moves people in a unified direction. In truth, the varied temperaments, maturity, and experiences become an advantage to the community, empowering and enabling them to move in that same direction while, at the same time, giving them permission for being at different places in that movement. Further, if people are allowed to be part of the decision-making process, the result is greater ownership for the vision and a growing maturity.

Leaders shape values and keep the goals before the congregation in such a way that people are mobilized and transformed. They realize that program development and numerical growth may be important, but they serve as only one measurement for effectiveness. Another important measurement is the appropriation of values and the implementation of vision that results in the tangible transformation of people into engaged and embedded participants. Together these people within the organization are able to develop new sets of impact and effectiveness indicators framed around the themes necessary for effective mission engagement. By nurturing the values inherent in the purpose and giving permission to act, leaders stimulate congregational and organizational action toward them.[19]

Servant Leaders Nurture Trust

People follow leaders they trust, and servant leaders nurture that trust so they can set the pace for the organization for needed change and the fulfillment of its mission. The atmosphere of permission and experimentation helps to stimulate vision and guides people into exploring new ideas. These attitudes allow congregations and organizations to navigate the white waters of change that are necessary for moving from ineffective and impotent strategies from the past to new and innovative strategies for the future.

The development of an atmosphere of encouragement, permission, and experimentation is a critical component in the servant leader's action plan. Combined with other components, such as the demonstration of commitment, attention to context, and renovation of constructs, servant leaders create safe places in which to participate.

The proof is in the lives of those around who are empowered and encouraged to participate. Their stories become the synergistic energy that creates momentum and direction. The stories of those being served as well those serving provide the letters of reference for what is taking place.

When Peter's daughter graduated from her university, she went with a group of classmates to serve in an AIDS orphanage in Cambodia. By her own admission she left as a slightly self-absorbed, and privileged white person. She returned with a profound sense of awe at the simple joy of washing a tiny child dying of this dreadful disease. She saw in the child's eyes what it meant to have someone love and serve. That was enough evidence for her.

Servant Leaders Lead from All Sides

Many people think that leadership takes place solely from the front. Servant leaders know that this is not the only place from which to influence. Paul's image of leadership as a father encouraging his children highlights this quality: "As you know, we dealt with each one of you like a father with his children, urging and encouraging you and pleading that you lead a life worthy of God, who calls you into his own kingdom and glory" (1 Thess. 2:11–12). This wonderful image describes three positions from which encouragement takes place: urging, pleading, and encouraging. Interestingly enough, these are words that contain particular positions of leading. Servant leaders know when to lead from the front. Other times they will walk alongside, sharing in the task, while at other times they will push others forward to enact and lead the task. They are attentive to which position is required at what time and in what particular context.

Visionary prophetic leadership at times moves out ahead of the congregation, "pleading" for renewed imagination for what might be for the church or their organization. Other times they "urge" from behind, pushing people along in the transformative journey or simply cheering as they watch others take up the task. At some point they will come alongside and walk with people as they take up the baton and move forward with ideas and visions that have emerged from within. They empower organizations by delegating or releasing appropriate authority at different stages of life in the organization while at the same time resourcing the possibilities so that others thrive in the tasks set before them.

Servant Leaders Lead from Their Own Ongoing Development

It is fascinating that Paul's image of the father encouraging his children comes at the end of his apologetic for his ministry among the Thessalonians. Visionary leadership does not occur simply because of a great idea, nor is it the result of a persuasive personality or a motivational speech. Paul appears to understand that prophetic, visionary leadership finds its ability to encourage people to something more because such leaders live grounded lives. They are secure in their identity, committed to the ongoing formation of a gentle spirit, kindness, and sensitive humility. From these places prophetic and visionary encouragement becomes possible because it finds its authority and influence from leaders who live deeply.

Leaders will never be secure enough to encourage others to become something more if they are fearful of being discovered. They will never take risks if, because of hiddenness, they are fearful of being found out. Leaders who are desperate for the praise of others will play to the crowd and shape their ministry to elicit affirmation rather than encouraging prophetic imagination. These leaders have too much to lose.

This is by no means a new concept. Leaders have always brought themselves to the task. It is an inescapable reality that Paul describes well as he speaks once again to the Thessalonians. Reflecting on his own ministry among them, he points out at the beginning of his letter a crucial observation: "You became imitators of us and of the Lord" (1 Thess. 1:6). The implication of this statement is foundational. Paul realized that people imitate or absorb the character of their leaders. He understood that leadership is, first of all, a question of character and substance long before it is a question of technique or skill. Fundamentally, the core question for a servant leader is "What do you want to clone?" And the corollary question is "What will you celebrate?"

The answers to these questions are telling in what they reveal about a leader's values and measurements of effectiveness. Working from a sense of self-awareness, servant leaders intentionally develop personal core values and characteristics that portray the kind of communities of faith they are called to form. Leaders must first model these characteristics before they are ever incarnated into congregational life. Charles Van Engen writes: "Merely developing authority – only telling what they should do and devising programs to do it, will not be enough to mobilize the people of God. The people must be shown a model that presses them to want to achieve those intentionally missionary goals of the congregation."[20]

Servant Leaders Love Those Served

Servant leaders believe those in their organization are worthy of being served. This may sound simple, but it is a profound insight. If the organization is thought of in mechanistic terms, the underlying assumption is that its members are somehow broken and need fixing. If the leader's main role is to help, the implication is that the members of the organization are helpless. When we elevate the relationship to one in which we serve, the implication is that the members are worthy of service and worthy of the time it takes to invite them to actually participate and contribute. Simon Sinek comments: "Leadership is not a license to do less; it is a responsibility to do more. And that's the trouble. Leadership takes work. It takes time and energy. The effects are not always easily measured and they are not always immediate. Leadership is always a commitment to human beings."[21]

Gary was engaged in a conversation with a gifted young pastor a few years ago that made the importance of loving people crystal clear. This pastor was describing his frustration with the small rural church he had recently come to lead. His presence in the church for only two years had borne little, if any, transformational fruit. His annoyance was expressed in the confident assurance that these people were not open to changes or worthy of his leadership. Gary listened as this young leader spewed his frustration with indignant self-righteousness. Finally, Gary interrupted his diatribe with a question: "Do you plan to stay long?"

The young leader looked incredulous, almost as if Gary had slapped him on the face with an obvious truth. "Of course not," he replied. "You know I grew up in the city. If a church in the city called me, I would take it in a heartbeat. Even if a call does not come, I will probably only stay three to four years."

This small rural congregation had come to accept that they would likely not ever be a pastor's first love. New seminary graduates would arrive itching to employ the latest ideas and church strategies which, the congregation intuitively knew, were designed to make them more of a trendy urban-like congregation, one more like the pastor hoped to lead. For years, this congregation had provided a place of warmth and acceptance for youthful exuberant pastoral leaders desirous to experiment as they learned their ministerial craft. This congregation had learned through the years of church life that there were two constants – clergy came and clergy went. Young seminarians implemented their ideas with little sensitivity or commitment to longevity. Worse, they rarely came as servants. They had no intention of sticking around to see their changes through and very little desire to serve the people they had come to lead. This particular pastoral leader wanted to experiment on the congregation too. It is no wonder that they resisted.

Servant leaders believe in the organizations they have come to lead. They listen because they care. Too often leaders fail in shaping the vision and creating the transformational atmosphere necessary for effective ministry in churches because they fail to identify with or sometimes even like the people they are leading. Martin Luther King was right when he said, "Whom you would change, you must first love."[22]

Becoming a Servant Leader

We began this chapter describing the kind of leader that organizations tend to request during consultations. The list of characteristics seems too good to be possible. We see the same list emerge as Peter asks his leadership students this question: "What defines great leaders for you?" In virtually every instance, the list includes the following. They:

- care about me as an individual
- are good communicators
- are great listeners
- have a clear vision for the future
- set high moral and ethical tone
- are passionate
- love to serve
- are empathetic
- are honest
- are authentic

These words and phrases mostly describe character traits rather than technical competence. Techniques can be taught, but the acquisition of character requires much more than instruction. Character has to be nurtured and formed; it must be lived out, incarnated day to day. It is character that enables leaders to inspire people and facilitate their transformation.

Becoming a servant leader is about people. It is about inspiring them to work toward something bigger than their own passions. Nothing changes in an organization unless people within the organization change. People change structures and systems. They make visions and possibilities realities. As Sinek writes:

> We need to build more organizations that prioritize the care of human beings. As leaders, it is our sole responsibility to protect our people and in turn, our people will protect each other and advance the organization together. As employees or members of the group, we need the courage to take care of each other when our leaders don't. And in doing so, we become the leaders we wish we had.[23]

The central concept remains the same. Servant leaders and the institutions they serve must be concerned for people more than for the fulfillment of the mission. They must acknowledge and embrace their role to ensure that those they serve, "while being served, become healthier, wiser, freer, more autonomous, (and) more likely themselves to become leaders" and to acknowledge their effect on the least privileged in society.[24]

3

Re-Visioning the Organizations
We Lead

*We need to move to an era in which leadership is an
organizational capability and not an individual characteristic
that a few individuals at the top of the organization have.*
  —Warren Bennis, Where Have All the Leaders Gone?

It is difficult to break old patterns. Part of the problem is that
we find it hard to see things differently. We need what Roger
von Oech calls *A Kick in the Seat of the Pants* or *A Whack on the
Side of the Head.*[1] In these two books, he explores ways we can
break out of the typical patterns of thinking we have used to
solve problems and even evaluate issues of the past.

Von Oech believes that we seldom have a need to think
outside the box. As a result, our thinking and doing are set and
patterned. When situations come up that require us to be more
creative, more flexible, many of us falter, even hit a wall and
retreat to old patterns of resistance. These blocks literally but
mostly unconsciously dictate how they will face a problem. They
will also at times determine the solutions. A friend of Gary's,
for example, when challenged by declining attendance in the
church over the years, had a patterned response: Leaders and

congregants simply had to work harder and visit more. In less complex times when attendance at church was strong, this "work hard visit more" approach proved successful. However, in times of religious ambivalence, his solution actually caused him to appear frenetic and naïve to the challenges he was facing. When circumstances change or situations seem resistant to our normal responses, we need to consider the possibility that our patterned responses are not the way to go. We need to be firmly committed to the belief that there are multiple ways of looking at a problem and we need to explore all of them. Von Oech calls this approach "mental flexibility" and writes:

> The hallmark of creative people is their mental flexibility. They are able to shift in and out of different types of thinking depending on the needs of the situation at hand. Sometimes, they're open and probing, at others, they're playful and off-the-wall. At still others, they're critical and fault-finding. And finally, they're doggedly persistent in striving to reach their goals.[2]

Von Oech is exploring a critical area that is an essential aspect of leadership today – the imagination and the ability to think outside the box. Neil Postman is often quoted as saying, "Children enter school as question marks and leave as periods."[3] He contends that the natural curiosity of children is stifled, even killed, by the educational methods our public schools employ. When those children grow up, they become employees and leaders in organizations but now with a fractured, stunted, or even crushed imagination. This is tragic on many levels, but when it comes to the matter of leadership, it is crippling. The ability to think more creatively is an essential quality of leaders and of servant leaders especially. This ability depends on our ability to recapture the magic power of the question. Good questions help open up the imaginations of people with whom we work and worship, and such questions are the tools of servant leaders.

One goal of good questions is to open us up to new vistas. Von Oech uses a helpful exercise to challenge us to ask the question of how we look at things.[4]

Gary has used this diagram numerous times in classes and workshops. Within it is a five-pointed star. Do you see it? Some people are able to identify the star right away. Others need a little help. Still others long to be able to see it, but the more they try, the more difficult it becomes. Some people eventually give up looking for the star.

The point is that sometimes the answers are right in front of us. Even though it is often difficult to look at things differently, our assumptions and definitions blind us to the ideas and possibilities they disallow. For instance, who said that the star ought to be just one shade? Or, how does one define what a perfect star is anyway? We bring our assumptions to every task.

This simple little exercise challenges the way we think, and it reveals how open we can be to possibilities. It also stands as an illustration of what might happen if you imagine different ways of seeing the church or the organization in which you work.

When the Lights Went On

Gary remembers the first time he heard Peter speak on leadership. It was during a time he was serving on the national board of a Christian ministry organization. Peter had come to introduce ideas about organizational change. His talk was timely. The organization was struggling to shape itself and live strategically into the changing paradigms of their current culture. They self-identified as a movement with a dynamic and energy as vibrant as it was in the past. But the organization's definitions did not match Gary's experience. Board meetings reminded him of that story of the psychologist who said to his patient, "I have good news and bad news. The good news is that you have a healthy self-image. The bad news is it is not based on reality."

The organization was struggling. They continued to function much like they had throughout their history. Without knowing it, they had become rigidly institutional and almost cultish in their protection of their heritage. Sadly, they were unable to see or acknowledge that this was the case.

Too often, board members represented the past. The corporate culture of this organization was sacred ground from which all were to navigate. Much of the organization's sacred history and commitments were held in mystery by those who had been part of that past. The operative assumption was that everyone should know that. Unarticulated assumptions meant that the outsider simply had to "learn their ways." Programs were evaluated, not on sustainability, but on memories of past glories. Talk of change was interpreted as an assault on the organization's history and a questioning of the effectiveness that had once been. No matter how this sacred history was framed, it became progressively more difficult to embrace the present and its challenges. The future was simply assumed to be more of what had been.

Enter Peter. He presented strange ideas about adaptive change and quantum theory. He proposed the idea that organizations can change from the inside out and that leadership is a facilitative/catalytic art rather than a command/control-management-by-objectives framework. It was difficult to assess the reaction in the room that night, but for Gary it was liberating. Peter was giving words to ideas that Gary had intuitively worked with for years. The forms and framework he unpacked were like an affirmation of what Gary had instinctually felt was right but had no words or models to which to point. During most of his career, Gary was constantly made to feel as if he was dancing to a different drummer, decidedly out of sync from others. Peter helped him see why.

Peter talked about great shifts that were sweeping through the worlds of organizations, including businesses and churches. Models of leadership that formed around hierarchy and bureaucracy were being replaced with new ideas of collaboration and connectivity. The outdated notion of aggressive management was giving way to the era of cooperative leadership.

This made sense. The shifts were observable. Companies that were taking the lead in thinking about these changes were giving up top-down control. By doing so, they were discovering that they could actually get more work done and be more effective. Things were changing, and Gary was beginning to realize that he was not as out of touch as he thought. With Peter's help, he was beginning to realize that it was all about how you see the organization and the metaphors you choose to lead by.

Metaphors That Shape Us

Metaphors are powerful.[5] We often use them unconsciously. They serve as lenses and filters through which we come to understand individuals, situations, or organizations. They also provide words that emerge from the metaphor, shaping the way we interpret and gain perspective.

Two paragraphs above, for example, we used the metaphor of "top-down." Here's another example: If you were to suggest to a group that one of their number, Bob, was a lion, you may hear Bob described as loud, brave, a hunter, or aggressive. On the other hand, a member of that same group may draw from that metaphor that Bob is one who rests or sleeps for long periods of the day. After all, that is what male lions typically do while they wait for the lionesses to deliver the prey. Regardless of which aspect of Bob's lion-like qualities come to mind, the more the group knows about lions, the more layers of interpretive meaning they are able to apply. By naming Bob a lion, we form a vivid image of him. These images and the definitions associated with them may be incomplete and potentially flawed, but they give us more information to work with than if we simply described Bob by his name.

Now consider the complexity of a university or postsecondary educational institution. The metaphors that describe different aspects of the organization will give meaning to its purpose and mission. They will also shape the way effectiveness is evaluated and how strategic directions are established. Students, support staff, administration, and faculty may function with differing metaphors. This will impact the way they evaluate effectiveness, success, and even their role within the organization. Whether functioning with different metaphors in one organization is problematic or not depends on the operative framework of the metaphor.

The metaphoric language we use to describe the task of leadership is critical because it will elicit specific understandings. If a president describes working with faculty as equivalent to the idea of "working with cats," that metaphor will elicit numerous descriptive understandings. If, on the other hand, she uses the image of "working with thoroughbreds," a profoundly different image will be elicited.

In addition to educational institutions, churches and other types of organizations also become prisoners of the operative image or metaphor that shapes their understanding of their mission or ministry. When Gary's mother complains that no one from the church visited his father when he was in the hospital, most of us would respond as though this was a terrible thing. However, we later discovered that actually numerous people from the church did visit, just not the pastor. It is clear that an operative metaphor is at work, and it contains within it evaluative measurements. Gary's mother images the church as a fellowship of care in which the pastor is the paid performer in the task of pastoral care. If the pastor does not show up at the hospital, then the church is not healthy or effective in its primary role as caregiver, and the pastor is not fulfilling his role effectively.

The operative metaphors at work in most congregations tend to be rooted in its history. Many a clergy-led change process has been thwarted because the assumed operative metaphors were not articulated, acknowledged, or even understood. In our experience, the operative metaphors may only have a superficial theological foundation, but still they hold incredible power. They shape everything from expectations, budgeting, ministry development, and even the evaluations of success. They also serve as a filter from which people can describe and convey expectations.

Gary was discussing the challenges a friend was facing in her congregation. She is an Anglican priest in a relatively established parish and had brought a vibrant vision and focus to the congregation. They had experienced a great influx of new people over the first few years of her tenure, and the congregational life had never been more dynamic. She was puzzled by the response of the long-time members of the congregation. For her, these were exciting times that represented an affirmation of her ministry and the work the leadership had undertaken to push out into the community. More and more, however, she was experiencing a sense of frustration and resistance. Established congregants appeared displeased and frustrated with the new people coming in and the changes they were bringing.

It did not take long to discover the root causes of this discontent. Long-term members held images of the church that elicited values reflected in words such as settled, steady, unchanging, and rooted. These words were being challenged by a missional metaphor that saw comfort and convenience as ineffectual results of a church unable to connect with its community.

This situation is no different for any other kind of organization. The complexity of an organization is directly related to the number of operative metaphorical images at work within the multidimensional and diverse places of relationships that make up the organization. These multiple and diverse images live under a canopy of an overarching metaphor that shapes planning and strategic direction, but they do not necessarily feed into one another. Sometimes they can even work against each other.

Images of the Church

Another exercise that Gary uses when working with congregations helps articulate the dominant metaphors at work. It emerges from Avery Dulles' research on primary images/models of the Church. He suggests that four operative definitions are at work in most congregations. Each image impacts our definitions and strategies.[6]

The first image is the **church as an institution** that functions as a cornerstone of society. The church as institution exists almost passively to serve as a moral conscious from the past, and its buildings represent a symbolic connection to and security of that reality. This image evokes a sense of having place in society and at the same time serving society as an anchor. Many mainline churches, still remembering the former position they held decades ago, continue to grasp tightly to this image.

The second image is the **church as a fellowship of people**. In this paradigm, the church is a gathering of people who come together for support, encouragement, growth, and love for one another. It is a place where everyone belongs and community is built. Its effectiveness is linked to the way members of this fellowship love and care for each other.

The third image that Dulles unpacks is the **church as a herald.** Here is the voice in the wilderness proclaiming the sinfulness of the world, its brokenness, and its need for God. Evangelism is the primary activity as the church seeks to "win people to Christ." The proclamation of the word is critical.

The fourth image is that of the **church as a servant.** Here the church is perceived as an agent of justice and mercy, and its primary concern is compassionate acts of care and mercy.

After identifying the images, the exercise Gary uses continues by having participants discuss and report on their responses to five simple questions:

- What sort of environment does the image suggest?
- What view of the gospel does the image suggest?
- What is the role of the church member in each image?

• What is the role of the minister/pastor/leadership?
• How is ministry perceived?

The discussions are always lively as those holding each of the four images of the church interact.

Images of Organizations

Gareth Morgan has suggested that all management theory is metaphor and that our images or metaphors of organizations shape how we think about what makes an organization effective.[7] Morgan's book is based on the premise that almost all our thinking about organizations is based on one or more of eight basic metaphors. He also points out the fact that most of our organizational conversations stay exclusively within one metaphor. Worse, he points out that most people are permanently stuck in their favorite metaphor and simply cannot understand things said within other metaphors because each metaphor actually has its own language. So each metaphor contains unique perspectives and is in fact cultural statements that have unique languages that animate them. In the scope of our book we will explore just two of these metaphors: that of the organization as a machine and as an organism.

The Organization as Machine

Images of organizations designed in a linear fashion operate like a machine. This mechanistic metaphor was introduced into management strategy in the early 20th century by Fredrick Taylor who is considered by many as the father of scientific management.[8] He strongly believed that workflow analysis and synthesis could lead to improved workforce efficiency and therefore to economic productivity. The emerging role of management was to design, assess, and improve workflow. Taylor and his associates studied how work was performed and its impact on productivity. His philosophy pivoted on the belief that making people work as hard as they could was not as efficient as optimizing the way the work was done.

In 1911, Taylor published *The Principles of Scientific Management*. He proposed that optimizing and simplifying jobs would increase workforce effectiveness. He also advanced the idea that workers and managers needed to cooperate with one another. This actually sounds humorous when you see it in writing today, but it was a radically different way of working than was typical for businesses up to that time. Factory managers had very little contact with the workers, often leaving them on their own to produce the necessary product. There was no standardization, and a worker's main motivation was often continued employment so there was no incentive to work as quickly or as efficiently as possible.

Taylor believed that all workers were motivated by money, so he promoted the idea of "a fair day's pay for a fair day's work." In other words, if a worker did not achieve enough in a day, he did not deserve to be paid as much as another worker who was highly productive. Taylor loved to study and calculate the time needed to execute the various elements of a task so that he could devise the best way to complete and compensate for that task.

This approach was eagerly embraced by people like Henry Ford at Ford Motor Company and Alfred Sloan at General Motors. They realized that they had a very complicated challenge on their hands. Their goal was to make automobiles and to do so with a largely unskilled workforce. They believed the answer to workforce productivity lay in breaking tasks into their simplest steps and then carefully supervising compliance. This is exactly what they did. What emerged was the modern-day factory assembly line.

A remarkable scene in the Charlie Chaplin movie *Modern Times* captures the implications of the assembly line. It shows that the result of a person being just a cog in the wheel or a piece of the machinery is mind-numbing. For those who grew up in or worked in that context, assembly-line workers felt as if they were no more than an expendable part.

Peter recently met a man who was employed at a large steel mill his entire work career. He lived an exemplary life in his community. He carried significant leadership and service responsibilities in sports, youth activities, and church. At work, however, his experience was profoundly different. He wryly commented during his conversation with Peter, "Every day for 27 years I went to work, parked my head and heart on a post at the main entrance, and then picked them up on my way out." His assessment is a tragic indictment of the pursuit of productivity in a highly prescribed, mechanistic world.

Unfortunately, we have seen similar approaches in organizations, including in churches and non-governmental organizations. The pastoral leader or CEO sees his or her vision as simply mobilizing the people to work efficiently toward the goal or stated mission – everyone with a place but not always a voice. As efficient as this approach may seem, it simply fails us when we move into a knowledge and innovation economy where success, however defined, demands that we tap into the discretionary energy of every member of the team.

Trapped in an industrial mindset, management becomes the task of separating the parts that make up the whole, analyzing them, and putting them together in an efficient framework. The assumption is that by understanding the workings of each piece, we will also understand and control the whole. This view of the world focuses on tasks rather than relationships, and function rather than purpose. Analysis leads to linear planning processes for a world we assume and desperately hope will be predictable.

The mechanistic organization functions on the assumption that our worlds are constant and without surprise. Frankly, this kind of world no longer exists in the 21st century. Just imagine how quickly the organizational strategic plans that were set on September 9, 2001 were drastically altered by the happenings on September 11, 2001.

The Organization as Organic

We are not the first, nor likely the last, to suggest that a better way of imaging an organization is as something organic.[9] In Peter's classes and workshops, he enjoys asking if there are gardeners in the room. For Gary, the idea of liking gardening is a foreign concept so he is always surprised when gardeners identify themselves as such. Peter asks the gardeners to describe what it is like to work a garden. They often offer statements such as these:

- Gardens are alive and ever changing and adapting often in ways you, as the gardener, cannot always predict.

- Growth is often unpredictable. You plant things where experience tells you they have the best opportunity to thrive, but, to your surprise, they don't. When moved, even just a little, they have a better chance.
- Elements of garden systems are highly interdependent; changes in one element of the system will likely generate changes for other elements of a system. Two plants grow happily together, but as one grows taller and leafier, it begins to literally overshadow the smaller plants around it. Something needs to change.
- Unpredictable elements, such as varying levels of sunshine, rain, and airborne particles, can throw off all of your plans.
- The goal is a harmonious whole, but it requires constant vigilance.

Each conversation sheds more light on the complexity of the process and the utter delight the gardener experiences when a flower starts to bloom. Participants quickly throw out concepts like control, productivity, and even detailed planning and begin to talk in terms of nurturing, wisdom born of experience, humility, and the sheer delight of seeing growth happen in ways that might never be expected. For many, the image of the organic feels like a much more comfortable metaphor.

Is it any wonder then that Scripture uses natural and organic metaphors to describe flourishing environments? We understand that sacred texts from other religions do the same. In John 15, Jesus describes himself as the vine and his followers as the branches. They draw their sustenance from the vine. Jesus talks about pruning and trimming always with the intent of getting the best possible outcome. Elsewhere, he speaks of his church as if it were a human body in which every part is vital and interdependent.

If we follow the path that opens up with this metaphor of the organic, we are moved to begin to explore the concept of organizations, not as well-oiled machines, but as complex, emergent systems in which:

- All the elements of the system are interdependent so any change in one element likely has implications for all elements of the system. For example, in a hospital, a seemingly small change in a procedure in the operating room can have often dramatic implications for other areas of service and support.

- Their existence is not in isolation but often nested within systems that are nested within systems, and so on. An outpatient clinic (where procedures that require no hospital stay are conducted) is part of a larger system (the hospital), which is part of a system (the larger health system) which, because of social determinants of health, are part of a larger, social system, etc.

- The ability to change itself is inherent. Emergent systems begin to self-organize in order to affect change when members of the system see opportunities for change based on their localized perspective. For example, a group of nurses were frustrated by their lack of awareness about the things that mattered to their patients. Everything seemed to revolve around clinical issues, and the nurses realized that they actually knew very little about their patients on a personal level. One of them, curious about whether other nurses in other hospitals experienced the same frustration, browsed the Internet. Her search demonstrated that they were not alone. She also discovered that a hospital in California had developed a way of bridging that gap. The hospital called it "My Story." It was a simple placemat-sized piece of paper with designated spots for such information as "The name I like to be called is…", "My favorite hobbies are…", "My favorite memory is…", and "I have _____ as pets." The group of nurses loved this idea and experimented with design, location, and process. They did not want to add to the amount of required charting, so they encouraged the patient or family to complete as much or as little of "My Story" as they chose. The paper was posted next to the patient's bed. That way, whenever someone came to their bedside, be they a nurse, a physiotherapist, or a housekeeper, they could look for points of connection with the patient. The nurses tested the process on two separate units and found significant improvement in reported patient satisfaction. Later, "My Story" was presented to the management of the hospital, and it was done so with all the gathered evidence of impact and cost breakdown. This was the first time anyone in management had heard of the system, but because of the nurses' efforts, it was adopted with immediate support as a hospital-wide initiative.

- Self-organization comes from the bottom up rather than top down. This process of self-organization is a characteristic of all complex adaptive systems and reflects an emergent process that is grassroots and not prescribed from the top down. Whenever you notice a group of people suddenly gather together on the street to watch a street performer or something that is happening out of the ordinary, you are seeing an example of bottom-up behavior. No one ordered them to gather, but each person stopped to watch, or chose not to stop, based on their individual choices at the time. It is difficult to predict what will catch their attention. For example, why is it that a particular church is suddenly hot and attendance rises quickly? Is someone in control of that process? Is it a movement of the Spirit or a word-of-mouth dissemination of information? As Malcolm Gladwell points out in *The Tipping Point*, when the number of people attracted to a phenomenon reaches critical mass, the phenomenon becomes a major fad or trend. None of that happens because of rules or external expectations, but because individuals make choices based on their own perspective and self-interest.[10]

A Disorienting Metaphor

One can understand how challenging it may be for leaders who are highly experienced in traditional approaches to management to shift perspectives. This is especially so if they know how to pull the old levers of success. This intensifies the disorienting dilemma for them.

Gary served in a global organization for a number of years and watched this shift taking place. When he started in his post, structures were neat and clean, and tasks were worked out in a world of distance and international borders. The challenge was struggling to find structures and procedures that worked in a borderless world of connection and quick response. It was not that the way of functioning in the past was wrong. It was simply that the world of that functioning no longer exists.

Our desire for predictability and order can near obsessiveness. Can it be fulfilled? It seems not. The world that functioned with precise rhythms no longer exists. Many would say it only existed in the past by rigid controls that often had violence or power at its foundational base. Leaders nurtured in that older system find it difficult to operate in the new world. Sometimes they are even resentful because, now that they have reached a place of position in the organization, the position does not hold the prestige it once did. In other cases, resistance to change is more an issue of control nurtured in the insecurities of a changing world.

An unpredictable world requires an organizational system that gives primary value to the relationships that exist between each of the elements within the system. Organic organizations do this. Unpredictable worlds require an all-hands-on-deck mentality which understands that we are in a constant framework of change that needs a response. Our daily responses to this discontinuously changing world shape and change us as well.

Every organization has the opportunity to honor relationships because every organization is made up of people. Organizations also have the capability to renew and regulate themselves so that the integrity of their core purpose is maintained. A new order emerges naturally out of fluctuation and a constant willingness to adjust and change.

Strategic Inflection Points

Numerous organizations have demonstrated their inability to adapt to changing environments around them. Many of them may not be well known because they do not garner the headlines. However, organizational failures that make front-page news show us what can happen when organizations are inflexible or change in ways that undermine their sustainability. On the other hand, the successful organizations have been alert to the need to reinvent themselves as the market changes. They have shown themselves able to recognize the times wherein change was necessary and then they made the changes that kept them moving forward. Andy Grove from Intel refers to these moments as "strategic inflection points."[11] Strategic inflection points illustrate what happens to a church, business, or other type of organization when it faces major shifts and changes in the environments from which it works out its mission. A new technology, such as the electronic tablet, enters the market for the first time; attitudinal shifts around a particular ethical or moral issue move from the back room to the front stage of acceptance; changes occur in regulatory laws; and the opening of national borders to free trade or simply a change in the customers' values preferences opens a new market. Each represents a major shift that can affect everything, and it can do so with rapid speed.

You may remember the handheld devices that were called Palm Pilots. They hit the market in the early 1990s. Gary can tell you the day that he threw out his day planner and embraced this new handheld device that could do such amazing things. There soon came a number of knock-offs, but he stayed loyal to his Palm Pilot until the day that he was introduced to a Blackberry. The Palm Treo was okay, but the Blackberry was enticing with its small keyboard. Some say that Palm's lack of attention to multimedia and pushing innovations forward, along with Microsoft's efforts to bring the desktop to your hand, resulted in the Palm Pilot's eventual demise. The company behind them missed the strategic inflection point. The rest is history.

Thirty-one. That is the number of months it took Palm to go from the darling to a mere shadow of itself. It now resides somewhere in obscurity within Hewlett Packard. Thirty-one months is just barely longer than a typical Canadian mobile phone contract. This was the pioneer of the Personal Digital Assistant (PDAs). They popularized smartphones and even developed a revolutionary new platform. But in thirty-one months, they were irrelevant. Understanding exactly how Palm could drive itself into irrelevance in such a short period of time will be a conversation for years to come. However, leadership is at the core. That, and a strange little device called the iPhone.

It is amazing to consider the fact that key leaders are often the last to recognize these strategic moments. Numerous studies have shown that these shifts and changes can often take place before the senior management even notice. Grove observes that it is often the "people in the trenches [who] are usually in touch with impending changes early."[12] This simple observation creates a critical implication for leaders. It is strategic to keep in touch with the grassroots of your organization.

When a strategic inflection point sweeps through an industry, the more an organizational participant is entrenched in the old structure, the more threatened it is by change. Consequently, the more reluctant it is to adapt to it. In fact, Grove observes that sometimes "the person who is the star of a previous era is often the last one to adapt to change, the last one to yield to logic of a strategic inflection point and tends to fall harder than most."[13]

The significant societal shift regarding lesbian, gay, bisexual, and transgender (LGBT) issues serves as an excellent example of this idea of strategic inflection points. Christian organizations desiring to respond to societal change seem to be acting with both indecisiveness and insecurity. World Vision USA came out with a statement that announced their desire to broaden their definition of which lifestyle orientation is permissible for their employees. Underestimating the negative response by parts of their consistency, more than 10,000 people dropped child sponsorship funding in just two days. World Vision USA then retracted their position and, as a result, faced the wrath from the other side of their constituency. It is a classic case study and illustrates clearly the challenge for leadership facing the inflection points of change.

This is where so many denominational organizations and older established Christian organizations and ministries find themselves today. Seminaries are reeling from the drastic shifts in their educational environment. Churches wake up to the fact that fewer and fewer people have the informed and natural inclination to attend church or even explore their spiritual journeys in what to them represents the religious establishment. For some organizations, change that will lead to their revitalization and renewal needed to happen years before; now it is too late. For others, it will require more than just a nip and tuck; significant change is required.

One final observation regarding moments of strategic inflection is critical. These moments are also the times when the arrogance and overconfidence of an organization can lead to its demise. This can be seen when churches or Christian organizations somehow rely on their God-ordained existence as being a guarantee for eternity. We must not live in this illusion.

Jim Collins calls this the "hubris of success."[14] He observed that many organizations can become isolated and even insulated by their success, and for a time can ride the tide of their success or effectiveness even when the environment around them is drastically changing. There are some fascinating examples of this in the megachurch movement in the United States. Such churches begin to act as if their success is an entitlement. They lose touch with the intentionality and passion that led to their effectiveness in the first place. They stop asking the penetrating questions that will enable them to be better or retool to be more effective.

Collins notes that the best leaders or organizations that he and his associates have observed appear to retain a sense of self-doubt, never presuming they have made it. It is almost as if these leaders harbor a sense that they may have just been lucky to get the results they did. We might say they never believe the press about their success. From a deeper sense of spiritual foundations, they have the humility to understand that anything that has come is the result of the grace of God. As Collins says, if you "succumb to hubris and attribute success to your own superior qualities (We deserve success because we're so good / so smart / so innovative / so amazing), there is a significant downside if you're wrong. You just might find yourself surprised and unprepared when you wake up to discover your vulnerabilities too late."[15]

The Leaders Organic Organizations Require

The psychiatrist Ron Heifetz is a compelling leadership scholar who observes the kind of leaders required for organic organizations. In essence, they are able to be present on the ground while also being able to view the dynamic from an elevated standpoint. The metaphor of the dance floor helps us understand that leaders of organic organizations are able to be on the dance floor and up on the balcony at the same time. These kinds of leaders are both participants and observers of the dance. In other words, they must be actively engaged in the daily ebb and flow of activity while at the same time able to elevate themselves to a place that allows them to notice the larger patterns and shifts in the system they lead.

Those who lead from the floor and the balcony will nurture organizations that are able to ride the waves of change, moving in new directions quickly. They are able to be fast, flexible, able to change directions on a dime, and remain nimble enough to continuously innovate. Ron Ashkenas points out that nimble organizations create boundaries that are permeable and flexible. Ashkenas identifies four boundaries.[16] Each boundary is described below.

- **Vertical**–*the boundary between levels and ranks of people.* When the vertical boundary is made more permeable, then position or office is less important than competence. The result is faster and better decision-making because it is closer to the action. Innovation and fresh ideas emerge from anywhere in the organization.
- **Horizontal**–*the boundary between functions and disciplines.* Increasing permeability of horizontal boundaries eliminates the silos that are so prevalent even in the smallest of congregations and organizations. Turf and territory are replaced by a deep concern for the seamless and effective functioning of the organization.
- **External**–*the boundary between the organization, its suppliers, competitors, customers, and regulators or accreditors*. In the new world we all face, the "we-they" of hierarchical systems and the "win–lose" of competitive systems must be replaced by the ability to explore possibilities of partnership, co-creating, and resource-sharing. Co-laboring and partnering create the possibilities of win-win situations for institutions that once saw themselves as competitors.

- **Geographical**–*the boundary between locations, cultures, and markets.* This boundary once seen as impenetrable has exploded in its possibilities. Online education, virtual classroom, satellite broadcasting, and various other innovations have rendered the borders obsolete. In post-secondary higher education alone, the possibility of studying at a highly respected institution without changing location is no longer an idea but a reality.

Becoming organic will not happen quickly. It will require hard work and discipline to revision the way we operate. It will also require confidence and security both within the leaders and the organizational culture to allow a variety of people, from inside and out, to shape and reshape the future. The ability to respond quickly will be joined with the openness to experiment. Such an approach also means that failure is part of the process. Leadership is critical to these processes in the way that Peter Drucker famously articulated many years ago: the art of leadership is to "get out of the way."[17]

Leaders of organic organizations create waves. Like pebbles thrown into a pond, they make ripples that affect the life of the organization in widening circles. Some leaders "cannon-ball," sending out splashing waves in their wake. Others are more like smooth stones that skip across the surface leaving little evidence of their presence. Whether ripples or splashes, the reality is that the effectiveness and health of an organization is directly related to the leaders who influence them.

Leaders of organic organizations do not function in isolation. There is a "we of me" in leadership today that requires a relational orientation not always required in the past. This does not diminish the significance of the leader's influence. It simply places it in the context of multiple relationships. It is also a characteristic of leadership that places greater responsibility on the leader to stay in touch with those he or she leads.

Perhaps offering a few images of leaders of organic organizations will give a clear picture as to the way leaders lead relationally.

One image is of the **leader as teacher**. In one of the great books on leadership, Max de Pree makes the observation that the first responsibility of any leader is to define reality.[18] Leaders may inspire and motivate, but the most important influence that they hold is their ability to actually help people achieve more accurate, insightful, and empowering views of the realities they face.

Peter Senge argues that leaders can influence people's view of reality at four levels: events (celebrations or gatherings where the new vision and values are affirmed), patterns of behavior (modeled by others and shaped by the new vision), systemic structures (the reframing of existing structures of responsibility in ways that point toward the new direction), and the purpose story (gathering of stories within the organization that illustrate the changes taking place). By and large, most managers and leaders tend to focus on the first two of these levels (and, under their influence, organizations do likewise). The leader as teacher in organic organizations attends to all four levels but focuses predominantly on the systemic structure and purpose. They teach people throughout the organization to do likewise. By doing this, everyone is able to see the big picture and even appreciate the forces of change affecting the organization's mission. They are also able to cultivate a sense of purpose and a vision for what might be. Because of their role of teaching within the leadership task, organic organizations are open to challenge due to the fact that they are interested in further improvement.

The **leader as educator** builds on the idea of teaching people how to achieve their vision. It is about fostering learning for everyone. So leaders working from this conceptual framework are constantly helping people learn about their organization, the worlds in which they live, and the ways of responding to the challenges. Without this atmosphere, leaders can lose their commitment to the truth and therefore relinquish their grasp on reality.[19] Leaders as educators, motivated by the desire to create a learning organization, know how to create and manage creative tension, especially around the gap between vision and reality.

Peter Senge argues that no leader has a more sweeping influence than the **leader as designer**, even though the functions of design are rarely visible.[20] The organization's policies, strategies, and systems are key areas of design, but leadership goes beyond this. The first task entails designing the governing ideas – the purpose, vision, and core values by which people should live. Building a shared vision is crucial early on as it "fosters a long-term orientation and an imperative for learning."[21] Other disciplines also need to be attended to, but just how they are to be approached is dependent upon the situation faced. In essence, the leader's task is designing the learning processes whereby people throughout the organization can deal productively with the critical issues they face and develop their mastery in the learning disciplines.[22]

The notion of **leader as steward** is explored by many writers and is captured in the idea of the purpose stories leaders tell about their organization. In many ways, leaders create the narratives that help people within the organization connect themselves to the big idea of why they do what they do. It is also the way that leaders help others understand why the organization needs to evolve and how that evolution is part of something larger.[23]

This is how leaders steward the vision. They tell the purpose stories and provide an integrating thread that gives meaning to all aspects of their work. The critical understanding is that stewardship involves a responsibility and commitment for the vision. It does not mean that the leaders own it. It is not their possession. Leaders are stewards of the vision. Their task is to manage it for the benefit of others. One writer calls this choosing service over self-interest.[24]

Leaders learn to see their vision as part of something bigger than themselves. These stories that give meaning evolve as they are being told. They give meaning to others because they emerge out of the organizations and the relationships that are at play within their systems. Effective leaders learn to listen to other people's stories and to tell their own as well. Telling the story in this way allows others to be involved and helps develop a vision that is both individual and shared.

Leadership in organic organizations has a deep commitment to what might be. And it also is able to live in the present with the not yet. This is a sacred tension from which healthy organizations and effective leaders act. It is the tension of the pastoral and prophetic role of congregational leadership. The prophetic side sets the boundaries of what God is calling us to. The priestly or pastoral side brings people into an atmosphere of grace and forgiveness. Susan Howatch, in her novel *Absolute Truths*, describes these two aspects well. The main character of her novel, an Anglican priest, captures the challenge when he observes, "There were two aspects to Christ's ministry, weren't there? The prophetic and the pastoral: He spoke out against sin but at the same time he behaved with compassion toward sinners. And he held those two aspects of ministry in perfect balance. But I haven't. I've emphasized the prophetic at the expense of the pastoral."[25]

Balance between vision (how things should be) and reality (how things are) requires an ability to live in the not yet without settling for it. "It is good enough" is never acceptable. After countless interviews and conversations with leadership teams and members of organizations, we believe acknowledging and functioning within this tension is an essential requirement for leadership today. Seeing the organization one leads as unfinished and in a constant desire to improve makes for an organizational culture that is dynamic and open to possibilities.

The Elephant in the Room

When we meet with organizations, we ask a series of three questions, the first one being, "Do you believe in continually asking the question, "Can we do this better?'" The majority of participants respond affirmatively.

We then ask the question as to whether or not the participants believe that the first question has implications for them and their church. Although the look is often one of confusion, most will again respond affirmatively.

The third question comes next: "Do you believe that improvement can happen without change?" This is where the fun begins. Many of the participants feel like they have been backed into a corner. This is especially so if they have been resistant to change. Eventually they answer yes, but generally with great reluctance.

The need to change is the elephant in the room. Everyone agrees that change needs to happen, but most people would like the change to look strangely like the way it is now. Most certainly do not want it to impact their lives. As one member of a congregation Gary once served said, "Why should I change? I have been here for 48 years. If they want to come to this church, then they can make the adjustments." The importance and nature of change is what we will focus on next.

4

What Has Changed about Change

Sudden shifts can happen in ways that surprise us; structures that appear as fixed and solid as the Berlin Wall can collapse or be dismantled in a very short time. An understanding of discontinuous change opens up a genuine sense of possibility.
—JOANNA MACY, ACTIVE HOPE

Mobilizing an organization to adapt its behaviors in order to thrive in new business environments is critical. Without such change, any company today would falter. Indeed, getting people to do adaptive work is the mark of leadership in a competitive world.
—RONALD HEIFETZ, THE WORK OF LEADERSHIP

Gary travelled to China with a group of colleagues from the international organization he was leading at the time. The entire experience was a wonderful time of cultural and political engagement. One particular joy was the conversations he had with the Chinese government official who accompanied the group throughout the tour. He was a graduate of the University of California, Berkley, with a PhD in economics. Gary and the guide found themselves in continuous dialogue regarding the relative merits of economic systems and the idea of globalization.

One day during their conversation, the tour guide chuckled and said, "You North Americans thought globalization was such a great idea. And it was … as long as you were the ones setting the rules." He listed several examples of how things are shifting, including noting the growth in the Indian and Chinese markets. He was right. The rules have changed. North America no longer controls them, and there are aspects of globalization that no longer appear as inviting as they once were. He proceeded to tell Gary a Chinese proverb: "When the window is opened, the fresh air comes in...but so do the bugs." This proverb illustrates so much about what is happening around us. Every innovation, progressive step forward, or new discovery brings with it a hopeful future, but it also brings the challenges of the bugs. Innovation brings new possibilities, but it also demands response. Innovation means that predictability or settling in is organizationally impossible. Change is inevitable.

Change is also not as simple as it once was. Peter has an American colleague who, in the early 1980s, was an engineer in the telephone industry. It was a time when significant change was occurring throughout the telephone industry in the United States. When the company was ready to implement a new nationwide system, the engineering team gathered at the labs in New Jersey. At 2:15 a.m., an hour at which they calculated would cause the least disruption, they threw the switch on a large wall-mounted light board. They watched the change fan out from New Jersey across the States until it reached California. It took precisely 12 minutes to fully complete the change. By all accounts, the implementation of the new system was a success.

Our lament is that change is just not that simple anymore. People do not have a USB port in the back of their heads through which engineers can reprogram everyone at the same time. It might work mechanistically, as in a software upload, but it does not work within organizations. Change today invariably involves people; therefore, it gets messy. It is often unpredictable. It seldom seems to take the nice, clean straight line that our project planning expertise would expect. Just think of the last time your current IT department told you that the new upgrade would not disrupt any functioning. The new operating system you were given was supposed to be easier, but with, and perhaps because of, human involvement, there will always be glitches.

Change Story: A Hospital

A few months after Peter left his position as the leader of the successful merger at the hospital, he was contacted by another hospital. Their senior management had heard that Peter had played a significant role in infusing a culture of collaboration, innovation, and shared leadership. They wanted him to do the same for them.

Peter saw an immediate opportunity. He realized that the change that took place in his previous place of employment did not emerge from a master plan. In fact, the plan for change emerged from within the organization itself. The results and improvements were obvious and significant, but there was no road map that he could lay out for the new client. There was no decision-making protocol that could serve as a template.

Within days of his arrival, Peter was asked to provide some workshops for approximately 80 people, each representing various departments throughout the hospital. These individuals had been identified as the informal leaders who could serve as communication champions. Their role was to act as an informal two-way conduit between the executive team and staff. They needed a range of communication skills, and, more importantly, they would represent people who had a real buy-in to the merger. The plan was obvious: these informal leaders would serve as the catalysts to get other people to come on side.

From this small initiative, a commitment to the idea of distributed leadership emerged. Rather than relying on rigid hierarchies and power structures to facilitate change, the idea was to create the context for a variety of local conversations that had some common ground in terms of the future of the organization. The conversations were highly localized and context-specific, guided by the communication champions who developed, over time, a personal commitment to the idea that change was possible.

This commitment to distributed leadership blossomed into an initiative called "1001 Leaders." The initiative engaged over 1,200 staff at all levels of the organization in a seven-week leadership program. It encouraged them to work on projects that had a direct impact on their day-to-day work. The executive team supported these projects and their implementation but did not try to direct or control them. No one project could be seen as "the one" that triggered change, but the sum total of hundreds of these smaller, local initiatives certainly led to a tipping point of change.

None of the projects were part of some master plan. Instead, they emerged out of the needs and opportunities that staff observed and which they felt they could impact. The leadership program encouraged relationships across the organization among people who might otherwise never meet. They were fueled by creative conversations among participants using language that was quite new for many. Cohorts were made up of managers and staff from all levels and locations. From the beginning, there was an intentional democratization of the process, encouraging all to participate and, perhaps more importantly, challenging managers to release their staff into the process.

Early on, Peter and others saw the need to crystalize the mission, values, and vision for the organization. In many organizations at that time, the Board and senior leadership developed this language in isolation from the rest of the organization and the community it was designed to serve. Non-participants dismissed such language as marketing material; consequently, buy-in was very low.

Peter intuitively decided on a different approach. He invited staff from across the organization to form a steering group to guide the development process. Over a period of several months, the group met to develop a framework. The group then took it back out to their colleagues and other stakeholders to get input and feedback. Steering group members then brought this feedback back to the group who assimilated it all into an emerging one-page document. The Board and senior team were treated as one of many constituent groups, important, but not more so than any other. In the end, a clear, compelling description of the organization's core commitments emerged, and a process was designed to formalize both the language and the level of commitment across the organization. For several years, posters could be seen throughout the organization proclaiming what were considered as the key guideposts for decisions, strategies, and behaviors. This approach has become quite common across organizations today, but at that time it was a radical way of implementing change.

In retrospect, Peter realized that what happened was a vital concept in the science of complexity – the clear definition of the system's boundaries.[1] These boundaries are both geographic and conceptual.

Geographically, the boundary was inclusive of two legacy organizations that reached across many conceptual boundaries: municipalities; ambulance, police, and fire services; cultural differences in the two neighborhoods that even had different area codes. Rather than thinking in terms of a merger of two organizations, the focus was on defining something that was significantly greater than the sum of the parts. That was the catalyst that shifted the thinking for people within the organization. All of sudden they were not immersed in either/or thinking– trying to choose between the processes and approaches of one organization or the other. Now the thinking had become much more "yes, and…" They were now drawing on the wisdom and experience of the two legacy organizations without any defensiveness or territorialism. This also allowed new staff who had no history with either organization to bring new ideas without appearing to choose sides. In fact, it allowed all participants to move toward being leaders in health innovation.

Conceptually, the boundaries that emerged became central to the decision-making processes of the organization. The mission and values allowed the organization to have a common framework within which to make choices. As the VP of Finance stressed at the time, strategy must drive budget – and that strategy flowed from the mission. When staff members from across the organization, beginning with their hiring and orientation, were aligned with the organization's values, there was a growing sense of confidence that they could and would make good decisions.

Change Story: A Church

Gary has a similar story of change that emerged out of the revitalization process of a once-proud downtown congregation he had come to serve. Programs and ministries emerged, but not from some elaborate planning process or master plan developed by the pastoral staff or the board of elders. Instead, they came from the places in which conversations took place and synergies were nurtured. These conversations emerged out of passions and commitment and ministries. Innovation was shaped enabling progressive stages toward renewal and revitalization. Even a growing sense of a confident identity as a congregation emerged as a consequence of those conversations.

One of the foundational frameworks that was used to bring ownership to the vision and the changes necessary to implement them were focus groups formed around the professions and circumstances in which individual members were engaged. Teachers came together with teachers, stay-at-home moms with other moms, lawyers with lawyers, retirees with other retirees–all with the expressed purpose of understanding and challenging members of the congregation to live into the worlds God had placed them. If the church was to move to a missional paradigm, it was critical that members of the congregation grasped a sense of call to where they were as a missional aspect of discipleship.

The groups met to discuss four questions. Staff members were there to listen and facilitate the conversation, not to participate. These were the questions:

1. What do you find particularly challenging about the occupation/circumstance that you find yourself in at this point of your life?
2. What are the joys and sense of fulfillment that emerge?
3. What are the ethical or moral issues?
4. What is the good news for people with whom you work, live, or relate to on a daily basis?

The conversations were lively. Out of them came many suggestions for what it might be like to shape the church in such a way as to allow these people to live dynamically in their worlds. The result was a commitment to the vision of the church that continues to this day.

Leadership was not inconsequential (nor was it in the context of Peter's example of the hospital). The change factor was not controlled; it was facilitated and nurtured. Input was invited, and an attitudinal change occurred that was the result of trust developed through the participation that took place. Diverse ideas and differences of opinion were invited, heard, and managed. The process was messy, but it somehow worked.

Start by Identifying the Nature of the Problem

We are aware of the propensity of some leaders to want to simplify problems so they appear solvable.[2] As comforting as that might feel in the moment, the results are too often simplistic solutions to what are, in fact, highly complex problems.

Brenda Zimmerman suggests that it might be useful to think in terms of three categories – *simple, complicated,* and *complex*.[3] A *simple problem* is similar to following a cooking recipe. Launching a rocket is **complicated**. Raising a child – particularly if you add a second child–is **complex**. The key difference between the three problems appears to be how one defines success.

When baking cookies, one takes careful note of the quality and quantity of the ingredients as well as the timing of their assembly. The assumption is that if you follow the recipe carefully, you will get good cookies each and every time.

Putting a rocket into space is clearly more complicated but may still be considered as linear. The difference is in the number of "recipes" or protocols and the level of expertise required. Success, however, can be reasonably predicted if you have a blueprint that both directs the development of the parts and specifies the relationship in which to assemble them. . The problem is clear: get the rocket launched, but not all of the solutions are clear to all participants.

Raising children is a significant leap from complicated. What does it mean to successfully raise a child? When does one think the parenting is finished? When and how does one measure success? The challenge, as with any complex situation, is that every child is unique, and one cannot separate the child from its context. In raising a child there is a constant state of uncertainty based on relationships between different people, experiences, and moments in time. If both the problem and solutions are uncertain and constantly changing, then one requires a highly adaptive mindset that is willing to challenge the notion that a complex situation will ever be static or finished.

The point is this: *Complicated systems* are all fully predictable. They are systems that contain formulas and procedures that, if followed, can lead to success. They are fully understandable because they can be taken apart and analyzed. From a management point of view, these systems are created by first designing the parts and then by putting them together. However, we cannot design and build a *complex adaptive system* from scratch and expect it to turn out exactly the way that was intended. These systems are complex because they contain multiple variables of interconnected parts. However, the positive attribute of these systems is that they are able to adapt to the context because they have the capacity to change and learn from experience.

There are a variety of examples of *complex adaptive systems*, even though they defy attempts to be defined in an engineered, prescribed, or mechanistic effort. They are complex because the systems can change through the interactions and relationships around them. They can be understood, and they can be influenced by a range of well-thought-out constructive interventions. Still, they are unpredictable. Some constructive interventions will fail as a matter of course. The most useful interventions emerge from within and will involve values that are becoming part of the system itself. The table on page 83 clarifies the differences between complicated and complex systems.[4]

In a *complicated system*, success is measured through cause and effect, and progress is measured much differently than in a complex system. In the latter, it is all about providing a focus and the atmosphere in which the various stakeholders in the organization can join together in conversations with a view to potentially change their practices to improve the way the wider system is functioning.

Complicated Systems *(like sending a rocket to the moon)*	Complex Adaptive Systems *(like raising a child)*
Formulae are critical and necessary.	Formulae have limited application.
Successfully sending one rocket increases assurance that the next launch will also be successful.	Raising one child provides experience but no assurance of success with the next.
High levels of expertise in a variety of fields are necessary for success.	Expertise can contribute but is neither necessary nor sufficient to ensure success.
Rockets are similar.	Every child is unique and must be understood as an individual – relationships are important.
There is a high degree of certainty of outcome.	Uncertainty of outcome remains.

The differences in these two systems are profound. The leader of a *complex system* requires a remarkable amount of inner strength and skill to allow it to function. Too often, leaders approach particular challenges with the illusion that it is simply a complicated issue when in truth it is profoundly complex. This is not surprising. We find our confidence in what we know, and we ground our security in living with the illusion that there is a road map, blueprint, and fixed signposts along the journey of change. None of us like to live with either the reality or the feeling that there is no road map. It seems much too risky and uncertain, even if someone promises that you might actually achieve the hoped-for outcomes. However, success breeds trust, and eventually it feels like it's worth the risk.

This was powerfully illustrated when Gary was leading an international mission and development agency. The organization was facing the incredible challenges of working with a partner in Rwanda and Kenya to address the issues faced by children who had experienced the loss of both parents through death from HIV/AIDS. Most organizations were simply dealing with this challenge of orphaned children as if it was a complicated issue. The response by many North American organizations has been to build orphanages. Building orphanages, however, did not make sense to the organization's African partners. The partners knew that without sustainability plans, orphanages became totally dependent on outsourced money from the Global North. These orphanages also created a problem when the child grew up: Where does a child go when he or she reaches adulthood without the inheritance of land? The land the child once owned had been forfeited when the move to the orphanage occurred. These issues and many more caused the African partner and the mission organization to see that the loss of parents to HIV/AIDS was a complex issue, much more nuanced and difficult than most North Americans had assumed.

What emerged was a solution that grew out of conversations with local leaders. It was an African solution to a very complex issue, and it was called "Guardians of Hope." The initiative involved the whole community. With mentoring and community support, children had the possibility of staying on the land their parents had owned prior to their death. This land was their future, and this solution was a grassroots movement.

When dealing with a complex system, it is better to start with smaller innovations (which Gary likes to call "mustard seed initiatives"). These smaller initiatives allow you to constantly evaluate and learn so that adjustments can take place. It was important for him to remember that he was not just working a plan; he was part of growing a movement. This is exactly what the African partners, with the assistance of the North American mission and development agency, did. Small Guardian of Hope initiatives were established. Over time, these same initiatives were evaluated with the express purpose of making them better.

This is the art of leadership in the 21st century—being able to identify the difference between what may appear as simple or complicated but is in truth much more complex. Discerning the difference will result in better solutions. Resisting our natural tendencies to want to control and allowing a more organic process to emerge within the complexity allows others to participate in the solutions as well.[5]

The art of leadership is having an array of approaches and being aware of when to use which approach. Most issues will have simple, complicated, and complex system types at work, and, in these disorienting times, there very well may be multiple systems involved at the same time.

Leadership Roles in the Two Systems

Complicated Systems	Complex Adaptive Systems
Role defining – setting job and task descriptions	Relationship building – working with patterns of interaction
Decision-making – finding the best choice	Sense making – collective interpretation
Tight structuring – using chain of command and prioritizing or limiting simple actions	Loose coupling – supporting communities of practice and adding more degrees of freedom
Knowing – deciding and telling others what to do	Learning – acting/learning/ planning at the same time
Staying the course – aligning and maintaining focus	Noticing emergent directions – building on what works

The stories of Gary's Chinese traveling companion and Peter's American colleague point to some of the defining attributes of *complex adaptive systems*. Understanding the key attributes that make up a *complex adaptive system* may make it easier to clearly understand why organizational change is so challenging.

From a people perspective, a *complex adaptive system* is a collection of individuals with freedom to act in ways that are not always totally predictable and whose actions are interconnected so that one person's actions change the context for other people.[6]

Another way to think of a *complex adaptive system* is as a large number of elements that interact in a dynamic way with a very high degree of information exchange. Interactions are rich, non-linear, and have limited range because there is no overarching framework that controls the flow of information. Systems operate far from equilibrium, which means they are constantly changing and adapting; the system is embedded in the context of its own histories.[7]

In summary, some of the characteristics of complex adaptive systems include: (1) they are made up of many agents who act and interact with each other in unpredictable ways; (2) they are sensitive to initial conditions; (3) they adjust their behavior in the aggregate in unpredictable ways; (4) they oscillate between stability and instability; and (5) they produce emergent actions when approaching uncertainty. [8]

Of Universities, NGOs, and Churches

All sorts of bells went off in Gary's thinking when Peter first described this idea of complex adaptive systems. The nearly 20 years Gary spent as a minister in downtown churches–which were in need of renewal and revitalization–were the crucible in which he cut his teeth on change management. More recently, his season at the helm of a medium-sized denominational mission organization has also brought new appreciation for how difficult change can be.

What he realized was how intuitively he had worked at recognizing the complexity of the organizations he was leading. He even found words and concepts for strategies and practices he had used in implementing change. He quickly grasped that the more complex the organization, the more critical this understanding of complex adaptive systems would be, especially if the task was to lead that organization through change.

The institution of higher education, a university and seminary of which he was President, was the most complex system that he had ever encountered. This 120-year-old educational institution had gone through a number of transitions over the years. It was facing three major changes as it entered the next chapter of its life and mission – a move to a new campus, the challenge of developing a new undergraduate university, and a changing environment in graduate theological education that had left many leaders in seminaries wringing their hands in wondering what needed to happen. Each challenge was complicated in its own way, but in combination, the changes needed were highly complex.

In addition to the complexity of all educational organizations was the intricacy of two profoundly different educational mandates for the two schools. From his initial conversations, he realized that faculty, staff, and students all carry different understandings of why the institution existed. Added to this was the traditional and grounded framework for faculty who saw themselves in the complexity of the academy as customers, stakeholders, and independent contractors.

Gary is still the President of this institution and continues to be fascinated by the environment and its intricacies. It is not uncommon for faculty to operate with a foundational assumption that the academy exists so that they might practice their craft. Administrative and support staff serve the institution, students, and faculty and, as a result, sometimes feel lost in the demands and assumptions of all those they serve. Administration is considered suspect by most, and the changing world of university education as a business (a word many of his colleagues find difficult to hear) is not always understood or, even worse, perceived as a conspiracy of the administration to foist change on unsuspecting professors. Added to the mix is the complexity of an educational institution where some faculty perceive themselves as uniquely isolated from the challenges of being an employee or at least an employee of difference.

To live in the illusion that the problems facing universities and educational institutions are simple and require only simple solutions is to live with a naiveté not unlike someone who decides to walk into a punch intentionally and willingly. This complexity was recently illustrated in Canada when a university, acting on what in any other organization would be considered insubordination, dismissed a senior Dean for speaking out against the decisions made by senior management, decisions in which he had been a participant. The reaction was deafening. National and social media quickly kicked into action, and the complex differences of a university and a business were clearly framed. Within one week, the Provost resigned and the President was forced to leave. What appeared to be a simple solution to the deficit budget challenges of the university, supposedly unleashed from on high, were tabled. The results were predictable: no solutions, no leadership, and a deficit that continues to grow.

Simple solutions are often the result of wanting to get to quick timelines and fast decisions. Complex organizations only move quickly in crisis. Academic institutions are highly complex and will not be altered by simple solutions.

Two Properties of Change: Emergence and Self-Organization

It is critical to understand two central concepts of complex adaptive systems – emergence and self-organization.

Let's consider emergence first. Writing on the topic of emergence, as one person put it, is "like clouds emerging from the physics and chemistry of water vapor – the concepts are fuzzy, shifting, dynamic things. They are constantly recombining and changing shape."[9] The new reality seems to be that, instead of being designed from the top down the way Peter's engineering friend would want to do it, organic systems always seem to emerge from the bottom up, from a population of much simpler systems.[10] This is why emergent change is so important to understand. Emergent properties are ones that are seen at one level of the organization but cannot be explained by understanding properties at other levels of the organization.[11] When change is emergent, we see outcomes appear in the form of new structures, patterns, or processes that were *unpredictable* from the components that created them.[12] Moreover, all manifestations of emergence are not of the same kind. Some are positive, while others are negative. Peter believes that positive emergence can be distinguished from negative emergence because positive emergence contributes to the mutual purposes of both leaders and followers who really want change to happen.[13]

The second concept so critical to understand in adaptive change is the idea of self-organization. Self-organization is a characteristic of all social systems. By recognizing it, we can begin to influence and facilitate better outcomes. Self-organization is the process by which people mutually adjust their behaviors in ways needed to cope with changing internal and external environmental demands.[14] Self-organization is a process whereby the organization or groups within it reorganize themselves spontaneously without input or influence from the environment, formal directive, or any external system. The fact is, self-organization takes place all the time, but we do not always recognize it, or for that matter, affirm it. The story of Kathy is illustrative.

A patient came into the hospital early for day surgery and was met in the lobby by Kathy, a housekeeper, who was busy vacuuming the carpets. Kathy recognized that the patient was in a somewhat agitated state, so she stopped what she was doing and asked if she could help. The patient explained why she was there and was clearly more than a little distressed at the thought of the impending surgery. Kathy walked with her to the appropriate elevator and gave her clear direction on how to find her way to the surgical unit. As the elevator door closed, Kathy smiled broadly and said, "Don't you worry, your surgery is going to go well today." The patient related how this calmed her down completely. The surgery went well.

Peter knows this story because it was told to him by the patient. He sought out to find Kathy so he could thank her for the obvious commitment she had to customer service. Kathy told Peter that she had learned from a nurse that cleanliness and friendliness actually have a significant impact on positive patient outcomes.

This conversation was, in and of itself, an encouraging sign. It was not normal for nurses and housekeepers to have these sorts of discussions, and it was obvious that the hospital's culture was beginning to change. At that time, differentiation of roles and relative status was clearly established. It was Kathy's final comment that stuck with Peter. She said, "In that moment, I realized that what I did, as insignificant as it may seem, could have a positive impact on the health of the individuals, families, and even communities we serve. I felt so good about my job!" Unconsciously, she was quoting verbatim the mission statement of the hospital, and her behaviors and choices clearly reflected the organization's values of patient-centered care and service excellence.

Kathy was not one who would need a great deal of supervision in the traditional sense. She had an intuitive understanding of the link between her work and the intent of the organization as a whole, and she acted accordingly. This is the concept of self-organization. No particular strategy had been codified or transferred from other organizations; it was process and an atmosphere that had been created in such a way that the changes emerged.

Order does not come about as a result of careful planning and effective execution. Rather, there seems to be an inherent capacity of living systems to find new forms of order. Kathy, the housekeeper, self-organized her own workload in response to the situation she saw in front of her. She recognized the day patient's anxiety and confusion and spoke and lived into it. Such interactions and choices happen all the time, and we usually take them for granted.

Our minds continually self-organize information, data, impressions, and experiences. There is no master neuron in the brain doing the work. In the same way, groups, organizations, projects, and even whole economies continually self-organize. There is an enormous potential for real systemic change inherent in the observable phenomenon of self-organization. It does, however, scare some leaders, especially those who are afraid of losing control.

Together, emergence and self-organization suggest an important phenomenon demonstrated through complexity theory. Emergent change is ongoing, continuous, and cumulative. Inherent in the term *self*-organization is the absence of a central design or control mechanism. In self-organizing systems, order–or perhaps more helpfully, *coherence*–comes from the actions of interdependent agents who exchange information, take actions, and continuously adapt to feedback about others' actions.[15] The search for new order is not imposed from outside the system's boundaries, nor is it imposed hierarchically from within the organization.

There is an enormous benefit to organizations that can develop the capacity for self-organization. It is our belief that the more self-organized the change in an organization, the higher the whole system's performance will be. Those individuals and groups in the organization own the change because when people self-organize around solutions and ideas they have helped create, they have a much higher degree of ownership for positive outcomes.

We know that allowing for emergent and self-organized change seems quite risky. It is especially challenging for leaders who have a high degree of need to control the outcomes. A place to begin is to think of a Kathy in your context and ask what it will take for her and the others in your organization to have the freedom to make choices based on their understanding of the intent and values of the system.

It is not a simple choice, but it is at the heart of the disorienting dilemma that many leaders face. Will we have the courage to let go? Will we face the overriding question that lies at the heart of this understanding of complexity – do leaders direct change and control future outcomes, or do they facilitate and nurture it? If leaders cannot envision and predict the future state of a complex system, and if they do not direct change in complex systems because it emerges from the interactions among people throughout the system – *then what do leaders do?* Here is the challenge for us all.

We know that churches and religious systems are going through monumental shifts. Global markets have made the world of business a very different place than it was 30 years ago. The only way those changes can be controlled in respect to outcomes is, it seems, through angry outbursts, violence, and power. Check the ethos of many church annual meetings these days.

The pastor of the multicultural church in the city of Toronto that Gary referred to earlier has watched the congregation triple in size. However, the old guard of Caucasian Anglo-Saxons is fighting every change. The pastor says that the reason is simple. The reality is that Toronto has become a much more complex place because of the significant immigration that has taken place. Many may wish it to go back to the way it was, but it will never be that way again. Searching for bottom up activity, allowing for emergence and self-organization, and nurturing an atmosphere of permission to find solutions from within will be the only way change will be owned and celebrated.

Get on the Balcony

In the last chapter, we described the metaphor of the dance floor and the balcony. Ronald A. Heifetz and Donald L. Laurie are the ones to suggest that leaders need to live with elevation. They have to be able to view patterns as if they were on a balcony.[16] If they find themselves too focused on the field of action, they will not be able to see the patterns that would allow change and innovation. While they give those with whom they work a strong connection to the history of the organization and what was good about their past, they nurture a sense of urgency about shaping the future.

Interestingly, these authors use examples of athletes such as "Magic" Johnson and Bobby Orr whose greatness emerged from their ability to play hard while keeping the whole game situation in mind. It was as if these athletes stood in a press box above the field of play while at the same time entered into the fray. It is a new skill for leaders, but it is absolutely essential in the complex worlds we find ourselves today.

There is no escaping the implications that all that we have discussed have on leaders. This new world of discontinuous change has caused leaders to swim in the waters of complexity. As a result, leaders who are stuck or insecure when it comes to change and adaptation will struggle. Leaders in this time balance a healthy sense of urgency with a deep and unsettling realization that ultimately the only control they have is over themselves. As Margaret Wheatley writes:

> Whenever we're trying to change a deeply structured belief system, everything in life is called into question: our relationships with loved ones, children, and colleagues; our relationships with authority and major institutions. One group of senior leaders, reflecting on the changes they've gone through, commented that the higher you are in the organization, the more change is required of you personally. Those who have led their organizations into new ways of organizing often say that the most important change was what occurred in themselves. Nothing would have changed in their organizations if they hadn't changed.[17]

> So the question is, Are you willing to change?

5

The Task: Leading Transformationally

To survive in the twenty-first century, we are going to
need a new generation of leaders–leaders, not managers.
The distinction is an important one. Leaders conquer the
context–the volatile, turbulent, ambiguous surroundings
that sometimes seem to conspire against us and will surely
suffocate us if we let them–while managers surrender to it.
  –WARREN BENNIS, MANAGING THE DREAM

Do not conform to the pattern of this world, but be
transformed by the renewing of your mind.
  –ROMANS 12:2, NIV

Peter made a disturbing discovery toward the end of his tenure as a vice-president at the hospital: he was not a very good executive or manager. This discovery precipitated his voluntary departure.

The senior leadership had asked Peter to expand his portfolio to include the supervision of all of Human Resources. This included occupational health and extended to volunteer support. He reluctantly agreed. The work was quite technical and bounded by policies, regulations, and union agreements. Since highly capable people were in place to drive the work, Peter felt some confidence in taking on this leadership task. But to his surprise and embarrassment, the work proved especially draining. He was suddenly engaged in endless meetings that appeared to him to accomplish nothing of any real substance. It was difficult for him to keep his composure. Basically, he hated the job and often found himself reacting inappropriately to seemingly minor issues. Everyone around him suffered because of his frustration. They wanted someone who shared their passion for the work they were doing, and it was clear that Peter was not that person.

In the middle of this purgatory called executive leadership, he attended a three-day training program at the American College of Healthcare Executives. The program included a battery of self-assessments and 360 degree evaluations. A measured career motivation test had a section entitled "general management." Peter's score was so low that he did not even appear on the graph. All of the assessments supported the same reality. Peter was simply not management material.

On the other hand, his scores on the leadership indicators were very different. The results were off the charts. It appeared that he was good at inspiring people to achieve great outcomes. He held the values of the organization high and was able to use them as a compass to frame all the decisions made within his departments. People were challenged to learn through his leadership and, in fact, modeled his passion for learning. One last outcome struck him: it showed that Peter truly cared deeply for the staff in the organization.

The conference concluded with a one-on-one meeting with a psychologist who reviewed all of the assessments. With a wry smile, after looking over the test measurements, she offered a simple query. "If I may ask," she said, "how long do you plan to be a healthcare executive?" Peter laughed and replied very quickly, "How long is this interview likely to last? Because that's how long I plan to be an executive."

He resigned. He informed his colleagues that he was determined to go back into consulting where he would have no one to manage and at the same time be able to work from his strengths.

The lesson he learned is that leaders are not gods and managers are not bureaucrats. There is a clear distinction between the two. They are both vital for healthy organizations, but they play different roles and focus on different aspects of the organization. They also require different skills. In North America, however, leadership is often valued more highly than management. Too often, the result is that excellent managers never feel settled or affirmed in the role for which they are best suited.

Disparaging comments are often spoken from both sides of the table:

"Thank God I am not a pencil pusher!"

"Vision is cheap. It is implementation that takes the hard work!"

"You managers always get in the way of the great ideas."

"He is a leader, which means that all he does is think up new ideas that we have to work out!"

Even the quotation from Bennis that opens this chapter appears to denigrate managers, characterizing them as people who hold things back or prevent things from happening. More recently, Bennis attempted to clarify the meaning of his previous quotation: "Managers do things right, while leaders do the right things."[1] Frankly, his clarification is not that helpful.

Do not be fooled. Every healthy organization requires a variety of skill sets and abilities – skill sets that function in an atmosphere of trust and affirmation. Organizations need gifted people who know that they need one another to be successful and effective. It is the synergistic entwining of the leader and the manager, the yin and the yang, that give organizations lift and leverage. Lift and leverage occur most readily when colleagues with very different gifts respect the other, understand the possibilities of a synergistic entwining, and work toward it. When this works, the organization hums with health.

It is rare to find both leadership and managerial skill sets in one individual. Managers tend to have their focus on the here and now. They make sure that organizational resources are being deployed with maximum benefit. Simply put, Bennis is right. Their job is to make sure things are done right. Leaders may focus on the right things, but invariably, they are unable to implement the ideas in the right way. They tend to focus on the future, but they need others around them to make the future a reality and keep the present humming along. In a time when adulation and respect are being given unrealistically to the visionary leader, we cannot make our point more strongly: leaders and managers need each other, and great leaders know this.

John Kotter argues that leadership and management are two unique and at the same time complementary roles in organizations. They need each other. Specifically, leaders anticipate change, whereas management is about coping with the complexity those changes bring.[2] For Kotter, the leadership process involves (a) vision casting for the organization; (b) nurturing alignment for people within the organization and the vision through communication; and (c) motivating people to action through empowerment and basic need fulfillment. The leadership process creates uncertainty and change in the organization, and the management process lines ducks up in a row so that the vision becomes flesh. Without management, the leader's vision is just a good idea.

Transformational versus Transactional Leadership

At some point, any conversation around the idea of transformational leadership arrives at a contrast with what some call a transactional leadership style. Peter is quick to say that transactional leaders are clearly the residue of the mechanistic age. It is also a style toward which millennials chafe and resist. So we will start with describing transactional leadership.

Gary remembers a young university student who came to work for the summer months with the organization he was leading at that time. Their conversation illustrates the resistance millennials have to this idea of the function of transactional leadership. The creative and bright student had signed on for a summer time-bound job, the task of which was to file. About three weeks into her employment, she confidently walked into Gary's office and plopped herself down on a chair next to his workstation. "I am not feeling fulfilled in this job!" she stated emphatically.

Gary admits to being taken back by her abrupt statement. His answer was brief. "I am sorry to hear that."

She then went on to unpack her statement, clearly explaining that she possessed the potential to lead the organization during the summer of her employment.

Finally, in exasperation, Gary stated the obvious. "I am not sure that your fulfillment is the purpose of this summer employment. You have been hired to do the job of filing for the summer so that you can make some money and go back to school."

What ensued was a delightful but odd conversation about what she had to offer the organization and how filing was demeaning to her abilities.

As the name implies, transactional leadership is contractual: "If you do your job, I will pay you." For long-term employment, it may even go a little further. "If you do your job well, then I will pay you more and maybe even promote you. Do it badly and I'll reprimand you or even fire you." There is little responsibility for the employee or volunteer to do anything other than what is required and doing it correctly. Everything works well as long as the leader and follower carry out their parts in the transactions as expected. Very little time is spent on vision, long-term goals, and strategies. It represents the assembly line model at its best, with an emphasis on stability, hierarchy, and clear responsibilities. Management and business schools have taken this idea of the transactional and made it quite complex in its implementation. The gist of it, however, is quite simple: It is a transaction.

To our amazement, transactional language still appears in conversation. Managers or even pastors angrily declare:

"They should just do it because it's their job! That's what I pay them for!"

"She needs to show up on Sunday and be more committed!"

These statements may be true factually, but they miss the mark completely in terms of motivating people. This sort of industrial age thinking, as Peter calls it, may have worked when work was predominantly manual, but today we need to engage the hearts and the minds of people.

Teachers know this about their students. If you cannot draw out the passion and excitement to learn, there is little left with which to motivate them. Parents think that teachers should just teach the subject and "make" their child learn, even though this same approach did not work for them at home.

We need to be able to draw out passion and creativity and tap into the deep well of discretionary energy that we all have when we are engaged in doing something we love. Simple transactions are not enough. They work for fewer and fewer people.

A much different approach to leadership is called transformative or transformational leadership. This concept has been the subject of endless study and evaluation. In fact, an analysis of key leadership journals indicates that one-third of the articles in *Leadership Quarterly* relate to transformational leadership.[3]

We are not interested in adding more to this statistic. Our desire is to help existing and emerging leaders contextualize and embody the identified themes in their congregations and organizations. What we can say with confidence is that the literature is very clear: Organizations that intentionally leverage the power of transformative leadership are more innovative and have significantly higher levels of engagement by their volunteers, congregational members, or employees.

Transformative leaders focus on motivation and formation, and they do it, not as a technique, but as a deep personal commitment. They see one of their primary roles as being mentors and coaches, helping others tap into their full potential. They make it possible for the whole person to show up.

Transformative Leaders Influence Attitudes and Atmosphere

Transformative leaders create the atmosphere, context, and support that enable and stimulate people to generate the needed transformational change. When the possibilities and giftedness of people are nurtured and when they are invited to be part of the vision and solutions to the challenges facing the organization, it is then and only then that the *culture* of the organization begins to adjust and adapt. When the culture of the organization changes, changes in the structures and processes will follow.

A management guru once said in an interview, "Culture eats strategy for breakfast." You can have the best plans, policies, or products, but without the right culture, nothing different will take place.

This has been illustrated in countless ways over the last 20 years in what Gary calls the "dance of the restructuring denominations." Denominational organizations have sought solutions in the midst of grappling with congregational decline and cultural and societal marginalization. The answer was often the perceived magic of structural changes. Jobs and titles were altered with the anticipated result being the revitalization of the denomination itself. We have watched countless denominations go through numerous structural changes in the belief that such changes would lead to new energy and purpose. Gary even knows one denomination that did this four times in a little over a decade. But each change turned out to be a futile attempt to stem the bleeding.

Restructuring made the denomination feel good. It gave them a false sense of security. They were doing something to address the challenges inherent in a progressively post-denominational world, and it felt reassuring to do so. It also kept them busy and distracted them from the real issues. Words were confidently spoken about the health and energy that would emerge from these new systems and structures. Confident presentations with artful PowerPoint® slides pointed to the renewal and revitalization of their life and mission. Key strategic shifts of program and focused strategic structures imposed from on high were supposed to lead to better congregational resourcing and the resulting denominational loyalty that had been lost. Even though numerous discussions and focus sessions took place, tragically, nothing changed.

A few years ago, Gary spent a weekend with a group of leaders of a denomination that had just gone through a deep structural change. The changes, however, had done nothing to stem the tide of decline, so they were meeting to discuss what should happen next. One of the denominational executives made the observation at the beginning of their weekend together that while the process leading up to implementing the new structures and job responsibilities was exciting, nothing had emerged positively out of the restructuring process. He wondered if it had been a mistake to ask the same people who worked in the old structures to implement and fill new jobs that were imposed on them.

The next day, Gary overheard a conversation in one of the subgroup discussions. In describing the restructuring process, one of the group members stated clearly and without remorse, "Yeah, they changed my job description and my title, but I am basically doing the same thing."

Structures and systems do not change organizations. People do. In fact, healthy systems emerge within organizations as they release and empower people to participate in the process of change. Structures and processes emerge from the conditions and atmospheres created by the people invited to be part of the solution in real and tangible ways. As the structures and processes begin to emerge, then the people who created them reach for even higher levels of performance to maximize what they own. It is like an upward cycle that draws more and more high-performance individuals to the organization. This is why they call it transformative leadership.

Transformative Leaders See People in 3D

Visualize each person in your organization as having three important and interdependent dimensions of themselves. One dimension is the technical and professional skills they bring to what they do. This is the stuff that shows up on our résumés. This dimension is important, and in many ways, it serves as a baseline for part of what they have to offer. It also includes the relational and self-management skills that individuals bring to the work they do.

The second dimension of the person is the personal self. There was a time in which personal and professional lives were segregated. It is really quite odd when people are asked a question or asked to do some sort of self-assessment and their first response is, "Do you want me to answer this from the framework of who I am at home or the way I am at work or at church?" It is as if they think they have compartmentalized pockets of brain cells that are activated in the specific environments. They may not acknowledge it, but people bring their whole selves to work, and the transformational leader gets to know and value the whole person. This also allows leaders the space within which to offer grace when an individual is experiencing difficulty at home. When you honor and respect the personal side of a person's life, while not becoming intrusive, you can earn a tremendous amount of loyalty.

The third dimension is the passionate self. This often appears with most clarity when a person, working from their strengths, is able to work in his or her sweet spot. Sometimes it emerges from surprising places. One hospital-based social worker Peter knew was asked to chair an accreditation committee. To his surprise, he absolutely loved the facilitating process. This was consistent with his skills as a social worker. When the accreditation review was over, he let it be known far and wide that he had found his new love and soon found himself in demand as a facilitator. He did not have to change his place of employment to do what he loved. He simply had to be given the opportunity to do it where he was. This is what transformative leaders look for. When they see it, they open up the doors of opportunity for people that allow them to do more of what they love more of the time.

The professional, the personal, and the passionate dimensions are the 3D of self. The transformative leader strives to help others draw these elements of themselves together not only for their personal and professional benefit but for the benefit of the organization. Bass and Avolio call this the "individualized consideration."[4] The leader creates a supportive environment by listening carefully, and showing confidence and trust by delegating new opportunities to people that align with their passions and skills, and then acts as a coach and mentor to help others become all that God created them to be. Transformative leaders nurture the giftedness of people and encourage an excitement about what they are doing and why they are doing it.

Leaders have a vital role in setting the direction of the organization, but they become transformational when they do that in collaboration with others so ownership for that future is widespread. When Martin Luther King Jr., articulated his dream, hundreds of thousands of people self-organized and transformed the culture of America. Bass and Avolio call this aspect of transformative leadership "idealized influence."[5]

Transformative Leaders Never Stop Trying to Innovate

Transformative leaders push people to their limits intellectually and professionally, but they do it in a way that is intensely other centered. They are not engaging in a form of manipulation. Rather, they have an honest desire to see the people they are pushing become all they can and want to be.

These leaders encourage innovation and value novelty in a safe-fail environment. In other words, they make it okay to try new things, experiment, make mistakes, and learn. They do this by challenging their own and others self-limiting beliefs. These are beliefs we hold about ourselves. We can hold them firmly and resolutely, even if other people perceive us quite differently. Gary is one of those kinds of people. The inner critic is always alive and well in his thoughts. It has taken years for him to learn not to cave to those self-limiting voices.

Gary was recently reminded about what had allowed him to lead confidently in the past decades. It was during a particular time of stress and discouragement. He was visiting with a person who has spoken deeply into his life spiritually. They had met together to discuss a retreat they were going to lead together. At one point in the conversation, Gary confessed his frustrations and thoughts of quitting. This dear Sister of the Sisters of Saint Joseph looked at him with gentle eyes and said, "You can't quit. You are the beloved of God and He has brought you to this place for this time." Her words were like a splash of cold water on a hot day. *Oh yeah*, he thought, *I am the beloved of God*. He realized that day that when he forgot this, he was no longer grounded, and the result was a fear of failure and a desire to escape the sense of despair.

Transformative Leaders Do Not Dwell on Problems But Look for Solutions

Good leaders also focus on opportunities rather than on barriers. We have heard reports of strategic research that was undertaken to measure what happened when a group of people was brought together to focus on the problems they were encountering. Results showed that, with this focus, the energy and attention in the group dropped rapidly. When a similar group was asked a similar question in a way that was opportunity focused, the exact opposite occurred.

Focusing on opportunities is not difficult. You basically acknowledge the problem you are facing and ask, "Given that we have this situation, what can we make of it? What's possible?" People follow other people because they are inspired to do so. Consequently, they are not overwhelmed by the challenges in front of them.

The transformative leader sets the bar high so that others feel challenged to achieve something really meaningful and purposeful. These sets of expectations give a sense of purpose and affirm an awareness that people today want to make a difference–they want to believe they are participating in something that matters. In practice, these leaders will use symbols and images to focus a group's efforts. Sports teams know this well. The sacred team logo, the motto, or the visual image is held up as the defining emphasis.

Simply challenging people, however, is not enough. Leaders must know how to celebrate success. They get excited about the team's performance and know how to affirm an individual's contributions. This inspirational motivation is a vital part of transformative leadership. However, it also exposes dangerous ground. What is the leader inspiring people to do?

Transformative Leaders Set Their Compass for the True North

Burns suggests that transformational leadership is a process by which both leaders and followers raise each other's levels of motivation *and* morality. This is a critical observation. Transformational leaders inspire people, but they do so with a sense of high ethical standards. We have often mistaken the charismatic leader's ability to inspire as something to aspire to. However, inspiration without character can be a destructive force. Motivational or inspirational leadership can be uncoupled from high ethical standards, but transformational leadership cannot be. Motivational leaders have an incredible ability to inspire people, but if they lack a sense of the True North of their values, they can lead others into the murky places of dishonest and corrupt practices. For instance, Adolf Hitler and Idi Amin were motivational leaders, but they were not transformative ones. They certainly could be described as charismatic, but it would be impossible to argue that they raised others to higher levels of morality.

Transformational leaders motivate as they adhere to foundational universal values and encourage others to do so as well. This is why such leaders place so much emphasis on ensuring that an organization's values are clearly articulated and then intentionally applied to all decisions and actions. They are also clear about the need for and establishment of accountability frameworks that help individuals, teams, and the whole organization maintain their moral compass heading.

Transformational leaders set the tone in terms of high moral and ethical standards. They know the True North of values from which they want to lead. As a result, they engender those same values in the organizations they serve. Hillary Clinton discussed this very point in a *Globe and Mail* newspaper interview. She suggested that when strategy and values do not align, you always go with your values and figure out how to live with the consequences.[6] People need to know that their leader can be counted on to do the right thing in difficult times.

When someone poisoned a bottle of Tylenol several years ago, the response was immediate. Products worth millions of dollars were pulled from the shelves. The President of Johnson & Johnson, the manufacturer of Tylenol, said, "Our first obligation is to the people who use our products." Not only did they make the decision to pull the product, but they made it from a core value that they would not alter.

Roy Disney, the brother of Walt Disney, is said to have once remarked, "Decisions are easy when the values are clear."[7] Conversely, we can think of many examples of individuals and organizations that have made decisions based on greed, expediency, and fear. Fortunately, most of these decisions are exposed, but often after the damage has been done.

Transformational leaders consistently make the valued decision and, by doing so, set the moral tone and value base of the organization.

Transformational leaders recruit, hire, and promote people based on their demonstrated alignment with the shared True North values of the organization. Regardless of role or position, they call people to work in alignment with the organization's values because they want every person who comes in contact with the organization to see those values in action.

When Gary was working with the mission organization of his denomination, he visited a church to present the work the organization was doing in India. Conversations over the weekend elicited excitement and commitment to the task of leadership development in a particular area of the country. However, in one conversation with leaders, he was told that the neighborhood around the church had drastically changed. In fact, a racist comment was used to describe the Southeast Asians who were moving into the neighborhood. "Those [racial slur] have moved in and it is not the same," they said. No one challenged the comment.

A $10,000 donation was presented to Gary for work in India at the end of the weekend. In the awkward silence of the moment, Gary received the check and then handed it back to the moderator of the church board. "I cannot receive this money for work in India," he said. "There would be no integrity for our organization if I took your money for India while you chose not to reach out with hospitality and care to the new Southeast Asians moving into your neighborhood." This was not a comfortable moment, but Gary had set the True North for the organization he was leading. If the church would not uphold the mission's values at home, there was no integrity in their financially supporting the mission for its work overseas.

Transformative Leaders Know Their Context

Leaders have the best perspective from which to see the dynamics of congregational cultural constructs. If they are willing to take the time to observe and analyze, their patience will be rewarded. Behaviors are a mirror image of the congregational beliefs at work, revealing what members hope for in the church and even in their own lives. Through these various behaviors, it is possible to discover the dynamics that are of greatest influence in the congregation. These behaviors are best discovered by developing the skills to probe and analyze. Leaders are able to discern which constructs are untouchable, which can remain without adverse effect, and which need renovation within the congregational culture. Leaders can do this because they take time to listen, engage, discern, and eventually challenge.

Gary learned this important lesson while serving as a pastor of an old downtown congregation. It was probably the most difficult time in his pastoral life. The church had become stuck in their assumptions; on the surface, they knew this. They wanted to change, but these faithful and wonderful people still held to the conviction that change ought to look remarkably like what had been before. The church had been in a steady decline for more than 25 years, but its members still held to the belief that all that was required was to do what they had always done, just better. They believed that Gary's role was to be winsome enough from the pulpit that people would come. This was, of course, ridiculous. The issues were much deeper than a cosmetic change of pastor. Many members had led years of rigid and lifeless faith. Many activities of church life were no longer relevant to the people they so desperately wanted to enter their sanctuary. The forms and rhythms were no longer replicable realities, and the worse part of it was the impact church life had had on their children. Many of them had watched as their children drifted away from church over the years either to other churches or from any church involvement at all. They grieved those losses but had never connected the dots to anything that they had done as a congregation. It was always someone's fault – a former pastor or some unfortunate sociological incident that took place that directly affected their life as a congregation. They were convinced that their decline was totally disconnected from the approach they took toward life in the church. Deep down inside they knew the truth of their situation, but they did not want to face its implications. It was asking too much to discover how painful this decline had been and to discern the disconnect they held from their circumstances and their own approach to congregational life. They knew that things needed to change, but they were frightened.

Looking at them with the compassionate understanding of hours spent in conversations about the church and their families, Gary finally asked them the question they did not want to hear. "Where are your children?" The question was painful but strategically critical. The question stung them. A silence fell over the group. He then went on to say that this is the crucial and important question that must be asked because it strikes at the root of the problem. If things are acceptable and as good as they thought, then why could they not reproduce that excitement in their children? "Why have your children left?"

The discussion that ensued that evening was a sacred time filled with moments of tears and painful admissions. But for the first time, these wonderful people broke out of the old unexamined and unquestioned constructs of their demise. They dealt with the hard question for the first time. Unknowingly, as they were challenging these assumptive beliefs, they were also beginning to look at what might need to happen differently.

Over and over again this same reality within churches, organizations, denominations, and institutions has been portrayed. If the real issues are not surfaced and challenged, they will continue to render the organization ineffective.

Transformative Leaders Understand the Metaphors We Construct

We have been emphasizing the idea that organizations, congregations included, are interconnected complex systems that function out of the embedded metaphors. They have the central characteristics of being both unpredictable and relational. They are places in which meaning and purpose have been constructed from within and framed around assumptions and habits. The key to moving them forward is the ability to question their assumptions and habits.

This can be powerfully illustrated from the framework of church congregations. Assumptive behaviors and practices that have been built up over long periods of time have usually been exercised within the life of the congregation to such an extent that they become almost impenetrable by outsiders. They serve as the unquestioned congregational mythology that undergirds the congregation's view of itself and its internal workings. They shape the views about outsiders and even about outsiders who come to belong. Over time, they form the systemic psyche of the church, weaving an intricate web of rules from which people respond automatically. Many processes and practices are lived out through habit. Over a period of time, they no longer require articulation by the faithful. Simple acquiescence is assumed.

If the assumptions go unchallenged, they become stuck and lead to an inability to move in new directions that might lead to a healthier and more dynamic mission and life. Before they can be challenged, however, they must first be understood. They must be artfully coaxed out of the congregational subconscious and brought to the surface so they can be discussed.

There is a wonderful story told about an airplane company that was struggling with the challenge of a model of a fighter jet that was simply too heavy. Engineers were sent back to the drawing board to find ways to reduce the jet's weight. One member of the design team bravely questioned the reason for needing steel frames in the headrests of the seats. To many in the room that day, this idea of taking the steel frames out of the headrests was a shocking suggestion. Every fighter plane they had ever produced had the steel frame embedded in the headrest. Nevertheless, the suggestion led to research being conducted on whether removing the steel frame would affect safety or purpose. Researchers found nothing until they studied some historic files on the history of fighter design. It was there they discovered that the reason for putting steel frames in the headrests dates back to the old fighter planes of World War I. The steel frames in the headrests were developed to protect the man sitting in the front seat piloting the plane from wayward bullets issued by the soldier sitting behind manning the machine gun. It had been years since anyone had questioned this assumption.

Learn *about the constructs.*

How do you learn to observe and listen intently enough to discover the deeper constructs at work in a congregation? It is not easy, and it is not natural. Edgar Schein, a MIT Professor of Management and author of *Organizational Culture and Leadership:*

A Dynamic View, contends that many of the problems confronting contemporary leaders can be traced to their inability to analyze and evaluate organizational cultures and the constructs that form them.[8] They try to implement new strategies, but along the way they discover that their strategies fail because they were unable to grasp the culture of the organization they serve.

Many clergy have the same experience. They come to their congregations with anticipation hoping to shake up the place. Some even feel a sense of entitlement around the implementation of sweeping changes that they believe are so obviously needed by their new congregational charge. Facing this impatient and uninformed leadership attitude, congregations invariably resist, not because they do not see the need for change or even desire it, but because they intuitively sense violence is about to take place around the cultural constructs that they hold as sacred. They may need to change, but they need to be first understood.

Change takes time. The deep transformational movement from the come-to orientation of churches shaped in the 20th century to go-to churches so crucial in the 21st century will take time as well. Nothing will happen without a healthy respect and understanding of the constructs at work in a particular congregation. Understanding and respecting their operative impact on a congregation, however, does not mean accepting their hold on a congregation and its ability to change and renew. It does, however, mean being aware of the power these factors hold in a church's life. They are not incidental and have taken, in many cases, years to be developed.

Identify *those who guard the constructs.*

One straightforward way to discover the constructs of a congregation or organization is by getting to know the keepers of the flame. They can be found in every organization or church. Not surprisingly, they are usually a small subgroup that has emerged over the years to serve as custodians of the community's constructed values and beliefs. Their ownership of these organizational assumptions is held in a way that no other group can, and they take their stewardship seriously.

These custodians are critical in any transformation process. Gaining their trust is often difficult because of the power they hold in the congregation and the unwavering sense that they are right in the convictions they steward. This reality makes them a formidable encounter. They may be well intended in their custodial role, but they are potentially dangerous resisters.

One organizational challenge that Gary faced was in a comment once made to him about how a particular department functioned within the organization he was leading. He was told in no uncertain terms that they were a "family" and therefore functioned accordingly. This term "family" sounded quite wonderful, but many families are extremely dysfunctional. Gary pointed this out to a barrage of passive aggressive resistance. Their chosen image allowed them to function as a silo and a righteous remnant in the midst of the changes they were encountering.

From a church perspective, this matter of protecting the constructs is not much different. In a small urban congregation, one faithful family serves as custodians of the constructs. This family actually oppresses the congregation with their foundational beliefs about the church and even about faith itself. Conversations with opposing perspectives are not allowed because this family is absolutely committed to the idea that there is no other way to see things. In truth, they would be appalled to think that some people in the congregation feel bullied in their conversations with them. After all, the family only wants what is best for the church.

The assumptions they steward are well articulated, but they are also unexamined in the light of changes in the neighborhood and the culture around them. It is as though these assumptions were built for another time and place that no longer exist. Those days were probably not as good in the past as assumed, but this does not deter the self-appointed custodians of the past and the cultural constructs that were created. This family has faced off with a succession of pastors and lay leaders over the years, holding to the sacred assumptions of which they have been mysteriously made custodians. Every pastoral leader attempted to confront the dissonance between the culture of the congregation and the challenges of the world around them. Several even saw some success, but each in turn experienced the brunt of passionately spoken words of resistance encased in scriptural references used as proof of their position. The words, too often taken out of context, have a way of creating an atmosphere of exclusion. Over a period of time, a quiet oppressive mood has descended over the congregation.

Custodial holders of the flame do not need to function on official boards or in senior management because their authority and influence are often informal. Leaders interested in new possibilities absorb the brunt of criticism through continuous subtle confrontations. The power to resist is an assumed entitlement by the subgroup; nobody has granted it, but, then again, nobody has successfully challenged the subgroup either.

Congregational members, fearful of confrontation, allow the dysfunctional behavior to continue. They do so not because they enjoy it or even affirm the foundations on which they are built. They are just afraid. The result is that frustrated leaders and new members become blocked from entering in. They eventually just drift away.

Smaller congregations are more susceptible to this custodial oppression. Large congregations have their own set of problems, but the smaller congregations are more accessible to the entrapment of an oppressive hold by a subgroup's custodial behavior over congregational life. Afraid of conflict and tension, unwilling to confront or support those who would challenge, they become a church ruled by a few and frustrating to many.

Congregational or organizational constructs express preferences for certain behaviors or certain outcomes. They are the norms that set out the behaviors accepted by others and the culturally acceptable ways of pursuing goals. If they are unhealthy and go unchallenged, they have an amazing resilience to continue in their destructiveness. Truthfully, if leadership lacks the courage or the patience to challenge these constructs, then vision and hope for a better future are pipe dream fantasies. It will take nerve to lead into the future.

Challenge *destructive constructs.*

If leaders are to serve as catalysts for transformation, they will need to alter the environmental conditions and constructs that are holding the congregation back. They must challenge the people they serve to radically reimage the assumptions, reinterpret the beliefs, and reframe the values that are presently at work by developing a process that establishes a new set of constructs from which a new existence can emerge.

Transformative Leaders Contextualize

One problem with the metaphor of the machine is that it is often disembodied from the place in which the leader is serving. It lacks a sense of place. Leadership is always giftedness in context. It requires a willingness on the part of the clergy leader or the leader of a different organization to express his or her giftedness with sensitivity to the ethos and context within which he or she has been called to lead.

In congregational life, the reality is that some leadership styles are inappropriate for a particular congregational expression while others are effectively congruent. Peter has witnessed the same phenomenon in organizations and hospitals. If leaders are unable to adapt to the context in which they are serving by appropriating a style that is suitably effective for their given situation, they will certainly struggle. If they are unwilling to adapt, they will encounter constant resistance and be unable to create the attitudinal and atmospheric qualities necessary to make the needed shifts toward health and effectiveness. Leaders unwilling or unaware of the need to adapt to contextual realities reveal not only a stubbornness concerning themselves but also a lack of commitment to the transformational changes they espouse.

Gary tells the story in a previous book of a mid-size neighborhood church that had filtered a succession of pastors through their congregational life. Each pastor entered his or her ministry with great hope and expectation. In each case, the congregation grew for a time attracting several residents who were intrigued with the new guy. The curiosity only lasted so long. Soon after the change in leadership occurred, the congregation stagnated. The decision by each pastor had been the same – to move the congregation into a regional church framework, one that would expand its purview from the immediate neighborhood to a citywide focus. The result was a succession of pastors who lived through the same frustrating narrative. Each pastor encountered a wall of resistance when the presentation of building plans and parking lot development clashed with the ethos of the people who made up the congregation. Proposed programs were rejected, and eventually the pastor left in frustration over the perceived unwillingness of the congregation to move beyond its seemingly insular mindset.

In reality, however, these people were not resistant to growth at all. Their hesitancy was toward the perceived impact of a congregational strategy that would move them from a parish framework to a more regional "drive to" church. Their church community was part of an established densely treed older suburb, and was perceived as the perfect place to raise children. The people who made up the congregation had great longevity and credibility in the neighborhood. Successive generations moved back into the same neighborhood because of the warm and inviting place it represented. Children, now grown, repeated the cycle, moving back into the neighborhood with their young families. Renovations and additions to existing houses in this trendy residential area were perceived a better option than moving out into the larger homes of newer suburbs. This was an established neighborhood with a particular reputation. And the congregants were fully involved in its activities.

Conversations with former pastoral leaders brought fascinating insights. One former pastor admitted a total incomprehension to the rhythmic behaviors so obviously inherent in this congregation he once served. This was a church absolutely committed to a parish mentality, and in his seven years of ministry among them, he had failed to comprehend how deeply this identity shaped their vision of themselves and their possibilities. Their contextual understanding of neighborhood and their life together as a church had been shaped for years by this reality. They were neither antigrowth, nor resistant to change. They were simply unable to envision regionalization of their church because they were intelligent enough to understand that it would not be consistent with the life rhythms of the residents and that it would divert the focus of the church from the place that mattered to them the most–their neighborhood.

Finally, a pastor arrived who understood the congregation and the community around it. He was someone who had been living in the community, who understood its rhythms, and who loved its blended complexity of people and community life. Together, pastor and people allowed the rhythms of the community to infiltrate the church. They became a church for the neighborhood. Its programs were set up to work for this congregation. Church program schedules accommodated neighborhood program schedules. Church members were encouraged to participate in neighborhood activities as service and ministry. The church building was opened up for community activities. The beliefs already at work in the congregation were encouraged to be understood as missional living. The leader who accepted this congruence of neighborhood and people set the congregation loose to be all they had hoped to be, having been given the permission to live it out.

Contextual leadership is sensitive leadership. It holds a tension between a respect for the way things are and a vision for the way things could be. It is in that tension and the sensitivity to the realities of the context that leaders find themselves within that mission and purpose are forged. It is the "we of me" that makes leadership such an art form and transformation so possible.

Foundational Practices for Transformational Servant Leadership

The Apostle Paul seems to describe this idea of transformational leadership as it is lived out in servanthood. With relentless commitment to the mission of the church, he fueled the movement of a ragtag group of followers. Oddly enough, he is not always perceived as a warmly relational historical figure. His writings, while ancient, remain amazingly contemporary in their awareness of edgy servant leadership.

He appears to understand the absolute significance of leadership being lived out in a particular context. He unpacks the set of practices that he lived out as a leader in the context of the Thessalonian church he began. We have noted that these practices are relational, and we believe they are the practices that open up possibilities for organizational transformation.

The first two chapters of 1 Thessalonians serve as Paul's description of his style of leadership when he served among the Thessalonians. At one point he describes the motivating fact from which he leads. He puts it this way: "So we cared for you. Because we loved you so much, we were delighted to share with you not only the gospel of God but our lives as well" (1 Thess. 2:8, NIV). This foundation is decidedly relational.

When Paul describes his approach to leadership this way, he exposes himself to assessment. He is saying that the evidence of his servant leadership is in the ways he demonstrates his love for those he leads. In other words, his actions tell the tale. Words are cheap. Actions are costly. If the actions do not support the words, then the words are rightly rejected. People who work within organizations know when they are respected and seen. If Paul's claims lacked actions of love and service, the people of Thessalonika could have called his description a lie. Their experience of his leadership would either legitimize the words he used to describe his leadership style or they would not.

This unveils the power of the relational servant model of leadership and its Achilles heel. If what leaders do subverts their words, their leadership will be undermined. How leadership is experienced either authenticates the words spoken or renders them disingenuous. We have seen many leaders through the years describe their leadership style in a public meeting among those they led and watched the look of disbelief. A leader's actions must match what he or she claims to be the case.

Lead with Groundedness

Gary had the privilege of studying under Dr. Archibald Hart at Fuller Seminary. One particular course focused on the interior emotional, psychological, and spiritual life of the minister. During one class session, he described the pastoral leader's life in the context of a diamond. Dr. Hart had grown up in South Africa and as a result used an illustration that was framed on the idea of life as a multifaceted diamond. He observed that too often leaders have lives that are "one dimensionally faceted." He observed that when we lack a "multifaceted" sense of self, an inordinate amount of pressure is placed on that solitary facet. Leaders who are not multidimensional are unhealthy. Healthy leaders multifacet their lives in the healthful conviction that when one area of their life is not going well, the other facets provide balance.

Edwin Friedman considers this same theme in a book that he wrote toward the end of his life entitled *A Failure of Nerve*. He observed that leadership has less to do with the specific problem, the nature of a particular technique, or the make-up of a given group. It has more to do with the way everyone frames the issues. He observed that effective and healthy leaders are well-differentiated people. He explains what he means by this:

> I mean someone who has clarity about his or her own life goals and therefore, someone who is less likely to become lost in the anxious emotional processes swirling about. I mean someone who can be separate while still remaining connected and therefore can maintain a modifying, non-anxious, and sometimes challenging presence. I mean someone who can manage his or her own reactivity to the automatic reactivity of others and therefore be able to take stands at the risk of displeasing. It is not as though some leaders can do this and some cannot. No one does this easily and most leaders can improve their capacity.[9]

Healthy and effective leadership cannot be simply discovered and learned as a set of techniques to implement. Effective leadership is a lifelong process of entwining techniques learned with the spiritual and emotional discipline that enables leaders to keep balance. Friedman believes that these spiritual and emotional disciplines are related to the individual's ability to become oneself. It is the ongoing process of grounding oneself so that leaders are not caught in the continual process of trying to assess, out of their own insecurity, where the others in the organization are at emotionally and relationally. Friedman believes that this place of differentiation enables the leader to find the capacity to take a stand in an intense emotional system, while at the same time control one's reaction to others who may feel more anxious in the changing situation.

Gary calls this leading with soul. Gordon MacDonald calls it leading from below the waterline issues of life. He writes:

> [T]he soul is the deeper part of all of us that others cannot see. It is a quiet place where people are most

apt to connect with God. In that deeper, quiet place of spiritual geography there was, in biblical times and is today, dialogue with heavenly events of repentance, praise ... and the formation of intentions to life and knowledge that enable people to become what I like to call kingdom builders.[10]

Interestingly enough, some secular writers refer to this as 'spiritual intelligence.'[11] They disconnect it from a religious context, and see it as a deep sense of connectedness to a larger purpose.

We see hints of the amazing capacities that God meant all of us to have as we secure ourselves in that resting place. It is the product of the indwelling Spirit of God that comes to replace the deadened parts of our own lives. Life below the waterline that is lived from the soul is just that – life.

Tragically, however, we too often pay lip service to the challenge of developing these characteristics. To live and lead healthfully in intense, ambiguous, disorienting contexts under-going massive unanticipated change, one must be strongly rooted. For Christian leaders, this means dwelling deeply in Christ.

Paul speaks to this rooting of identity in Christ in his letter to the Colossians. In describing the characteristics of community living (Col. 3:12ff) after a long teaching in the first two chapters around the character of Jesus, he moves to a practical conversation about how we live as a community called the church. He calls the church to live out that experience of Christ–being relational, forgiving, patient with each other, and gentle as they live together. Before he describes these characteristics, he first comments on the prerequisite convictions necessary for the community living he describes. You must know that you are holy, chosen, and dearly loved by God (3:12).

Lead from Who You Are

We have come to realize after years of observation and consultation with leaders in both the church and nonchurch worlds that whatever else we bring to the table as a leader, we ultimately bring ourselves. Our personal narrative shapes the way we lead. Our lived experience is the filter through which our leadership emerges.

We live in a country that negatively images aggressive and proactive leadership. Canadians like their leaders to be somewhat reluctant and unassuming. While we Canadians covet the "can do" atmosphere so prevalent in the States, we prefer a less forceful quality. This view of leadership is shaped by our history and the way we grew up in Canada. Our history and culture influence everything we do and even the way we treat leaders with imputed positional authority.

What we have learned about ourselves is true for all of us. Leaders' personal narratives are never far away from the way they lead. They either do so with a sense of self-awareness or self-deception. Jim Clemmer quotes management consultants Lee Bolman and Terence Deal, who say that "The signs point toward spirit and soul as the essence of leadership."[12] If we ignore our personal stories, the result is a strangely hollow leader, someone who spends most of life ministering and leading as though he or she is simply responding to events and circumstances, rather than influencing and leading in them.

Living from the soul of leadership, that is, the place of self-awareness which nurtures from below the waterline issues of life, provides a place from which quality leadership and transformative adaptive change are possible. Leaders become more influential because their soul capacity creates a grounded place of sureness from which they can find courage to risk, share power, and allow others to participate. Without this capacity, life is shallow, and the nerve to lead is almost impossible to conjure up. The result of leadership from within is a leadership style more rooted in character development than learned technical skills. Inner development of character focused on themes such as integrity, honesty, humility, courage, commitment, sincerity, passion, confidence, wisdom, determination, compassion, and sensitivity, are crucial.

Who we are and who we see ourselves to be are crucial to leadership. We bring ourselves, our coping skills, relational ability, approach to faith, values, and even our sense of worth to leadership roles. Gary's friend and colleague, Brian Craig, reflects on this truth through sharing his personal narrative:

Through much of my life, I've been what could be called a "reluctant leader." I never could see myself in the faces of the charismatic, inspiring leaders who had been served up as models in my earlier life by the prevailing culture around me. War heroes, sports legends, and even the great civil rights leaders who filled the pages of newspapers in my childhood had nothing to do with me. I could do all sorts of things fairly well – music, theatre, math and science stuff, even public speaking, but none of those activities were 'leading' in my mind.

By the time I somehow found myself understanding a call to ministry, I still would not have used the term leader for myself. I was a teacher, a pastor, a preacher, but leader? No, not me. A new generation of Christian leaders had arisen and some were saying things like (or so I heard them say), "If you don't have the gift of visionary leadership, get out of the ministry." I knew that was not me. I once heard someone quip, "Moses went up the mountain and came down with the tablets of the Law; I go up and come down with the tablets of the Tylenol." I felt I had found a life motto.

But somehow, God's understanding of leadership was not what I had been hearing all along. His work in my story has been to convince me that the vision of leadership I had bought, as being only about charisma and flare and the big moment, was, theologically speaking, a load of hooey. When God invited me to lead others, God was not surprised by the gifts and abilities I had. God asked me to step into leadership *because* of how he had gifted me. In fact, those gifts were exactly the way he wanted me to lead. In using the word "gift," I am not simply talking about "spiritual gifts" in the biblical sense. The way God wired me, the way he put me together, the abilities and strengths he has placed in me, even the gaps and struggles – all these are his work in my life. And from that raw material, he asks me to lead.

Along the way, with what I believe is a sense of humour, God has now allowed me to work with others, to help them grow in their ability to lead. And the punchline of that long story is what I hope they will see. **Lead because of who you are.** Don't lead trying to be someone else. Lead out of your strengths, as you are gifted. Lead that way.[13]

Lead Transparently

Effective leaders ultimately distinguish themselves by their ability to inspire followers to commit passionately to the cause. Jimmy Long writes, "We need to make sure that we create an environment in our churches and our Christian fellowships that allow people to become vulnerable enough to share their pain and struggles."[14] By taking a "what you see is what you get" code of conduct, leaders show respect to the people they are leading and model the possibilities of transparency and honest sharing in the community of faith. This creates credibility and cultivates fertile ground for effective collaboration.

True leadership is built on the type of social contract that says, "Follow me, and I promise that I will help you become something more." If congregations are led to wonder about the hidden agendas of their leaders, then the distrust that results will have a negative impact on the life of the community of faith. Paul is absolutely emphatic about his motives for leadership. He describes his leadership among the Thessalonians as not having been exercised with "from 'deceit or impure motives or trickery" (1 Thess. 2:3). While it is crucial to know how far to go as you transparently open yourself up as a leader to the congregation, congregations that see nothing of the leader as a fellow human being among them follow their leadership with great reluctance. The reason is simple – people's expectations for leadership are rooted in the basic interpersonal operation of leader-follower relationships. When personal connections are not made through trust, reliability, care, and appreciation, there is little opportunity for the community to move to a higher level of effectiveness and deeper lives of care.

Congregations desiring genuine engagement in their communities and rediscovery of the dynamic of a living, breathing community of faith in all its messiness must work to build genuine community themselves. Strategies and change emerge through transparent and honest relationships. Genuine community challenges the individualistic tendencies of North American culture. God created us for community, not for disingenuous relationships of insecure needs and aspirations.

Lead from a Humble Sensibility

Genuinely communal and transparent living is nurtured most effectively through leaders who approach their task with humble sensibility. Paul speaks to this character attribute as he describes his ministry. It did not emerge from the deep hollowness of ego needs or the shallowness of playing to the crowd for praise and flattery (1 Thess. 2:5).

Everyone needs encouragement and is encouraged by affirmation. However, the most destructive relationships are built by people who need affirmation too much. This insatiable need for emotional strokes is a signal of a leader's insecurity which, if not checked, results in an emotional entrapment of leaders to the whim of people around them. The already fragile and vulnerable nature of leadership or pastoral ministry creates an even more destructive trap when wrapped in this need for encouragement or strokes.

Emotionally dependent leaders will not risk themselves enough to be prophetic in their organizations or their congregations. When they choose the prophetic role, too often they are playing to the crowd, which is a corruption of that role.

Approaching leadership with humble sensibility allows the leader to find vision, strength, and creativity within the community of faith. Humble sensibility allows the leader to see people, not as the consumer, but as people who are also seeking a vision for the church and people who also bring gifts to the leadership task. It continues to empower the communal nature of leadership in the church where community building is part of the kingdom-shaping task for the church's mission.

Lead Sensitively

Effective leaders bring a character that is sensitive to the task. Paul aptly describes this sensitivity when he tells the Thessalonians that he and his ministry colleagues were gentle among the people of Thessalonika, in the way a mother nurtures or nurses her infant (1 Thess. 2:7). It's a wonderful image capturing the idea of intimacy and strength. The idea of gentleness in the scriptures is always linked to this concept of controlled strength. Paul's comparison of gentleness to the image of a nursing mother illustrates this dual nature–the hungry infant suckling with eagerness while the mother gently coos to her child with calm assurance.

The numerous scriptural references to words like patience, longsuffering, and steadfastness portray the quality of relationships possible as a gospel people. They also paint a picture of the character required to lead any organization. Organizations and churches are communities of ordinary people carrying varied agendas. Leadership sensitively nurtures this diversity by knowing when to push and when to lay back on issues. Leaders are able to discern the battles that must be fought and those that can be ignored. Patient-sensitive ministry envisions long-term possibilities and therefore creates an environment for growth.

As we read many books that deal with leadership in the 21st century, we were amazed to realize that they point back at this specific practice of leading sensitively as being critical to effective organizational and congregational mission accomplishment. Sensitive leaders shun celebrity and channel their ambition toward building a great organization. They have unwavering resolve and lead with a sensibility that is rooted in humility and the desire to see everyone help them fulfill the mission of the organization.

The leadership characteristics of humble sensibility and sensitivity enable leaders to gain clarity as they observe their congregation or organization. They are able to respond quickly as shifts and turns take place in one part of the organization. They are able do so because they are secure enough not to be affected by the challenges and problems that surface.

Such leaders are also not easily frozen by emotional isolation used by some for manipulation and resistance. Their informed insight about people empowers their ability to navigate through and negotiate the ebbs and flows that are natural in the life of an organization. It is obvious to them that vision and possibilities emerge from the organization and not just the leaders, so they look for those possibilities in others.

Ultimately, these kinds of leaders are community builders. They draw vision, giftedness, and relationships out of the community while warring against the tendency toward going it on their own. In this cultivated atmosphere, the imagination of members emerges in greater clarity. It is a vision that does not come from preplanned strategies void of dialogue or process, but from the community's shared experience and God moving in the midst of the community itself. It is revealed, not by manipulation, but through listening and discernment. These leaders are open to the opinions of others and to a vision that emerges from them. While this approach to leadership is not natural for many, it can be learned, and it is an essential ingredient necessary for both shaping and creating ownership for the vision.

6

The Rock, the Bird, and the Bucket

The notion that the only way you can critically engage with a person's ideas is to take a shot at them, is to be openly critical– this is actually nonsense. Some of the most effective ways in which you deal with someone's ideas are to treat them completely at face value, and with an enormous amount of respect. That's actually a faster way to engage with what they're getting at than to lob grenades in their direction…

—MALCOLM GLADWELL, DAVID AND GOLIATH

That's your responsibility as a person, as a human being – to constantly be updating your position on as many things as possible. And if you don't contradict yourself on a regular basis, then you're not thinking.

—MALCOLM GLADWELL, DAVID AND GOLIATH

If your actions inspire others to dream more, learn more, do more and become more, you are a leader. It is not the genius at the top giving directions that makes people great. It is great people that make the guy at the top look like a genius.

—SIMON SINEK, LEADERS EAT LAST

If you want to toss a rock into a bucket from 20 feet away with 90 percent accuracy, what would it take? Generally speaking, it requires a working knowledge of physics reinforced by the development of muscle memory. Consciously or not, you would calculate the velocity, trajectory, angle of release, and requisite mechanics. Then, throw after throw you would hone your skills. The skill of being able to throw a rock into a bucket is a matter of sheer repetitive practice.

But what do you do when the object you are throwing is not something inanimate like a rock but a free agent, say, a bird? Getting the bird into the bucket is no longer a simple matter of target practice because, once released, the bird will fly away. The odds of it going where you want it to go are slim to none.

People are like birds. Unlike rocks and baseballs, they have minds of their own, wills of their own, and the freedom to choose to fly or not to fly into the bucket. This is another reason why the metaphor of organizations as machines is especially problematic to leaders today. It conjures up the image of people as extensions of the machine and leaders as the people who figure out the right way to plug them in so that things can run as they always have. This metaphor falls flat because it fails to recognize human nature, our intrinsic resentment toward coercion, and our dissatisfaction with being just another cog in the machinery.

Peter enjoys using this rock-bird metaphor in workshop settings. It always elicits fascinating discussions. The most fun comes when he asks the question, "How would you get the bird into the bucket?" Inevitably, people start to snicker and say things like, "Well, I suppose you'd have to knock the bird unconscious." Others recommend less drastic solutions, such as "Wrap it in duct tape so that it's still conscious but unable to fly." One of Peter's favorite answers was from someone who worked in Human Resources who said, "Well, we would build an invisible tunnel to the bucket made out of a set of infallible policies and procedures so while the bird thought it was free, it really had nowhere else to go but to the bucket."

To find the real answer, of course, we need to rephrase the question. Instead of asking, "How do you get the bird to the bucket?" we need to ask, "How do you attract the bird to the bucket?" The answer lies in finding the right birdseed.

The beauty of birdseed is twofold. First, you can attract the bird to the bucket without much effort. And second, by choosing a particular variety of birdseed, you can attract a specific kind of bird. This is helpful given the fact that we are dealing with a diversity of people. Leaders need a combination of several attractors to motivate people to the bucket. It is these attractors that we have attempted to identify in the preceding chapters. By way of review and summary, we offer the following sections to highlight those we consider the key concepts of learning about leadership.

Birds to Buckets Is a Complex Process

Nine years ago, Peter was diagnosed and treated for a malignant solid mass tumor at the base of his tongue. The treatment of this disease became his "up close and personal experience" with healthcare as a complex adaptive system. One oncologist said to Peter, "Treating cancer is complex because the disease is not exactly the same in each patient and because no patient responds the same way to the treatment." The complexity increases as one considers the numerous people involved with the process, each with their own individual complexities as well. Peter's treatment was an example of emergent change and unpredictable outcomes. He had to grow in comfort with the reality that there was no clarity or certainty of outcome and that the strategies and approaches were constantly changing. Treatment protocols were, in some cases, relatively novel and unique.

Clearly, the system of care delivery is both complex and adaptive. Upon reflection, three characteristics signify just how complex Peter's treatment process really was.

1. **Agents:** There were multiple individuals who played vital roles acting and reacting within the context of treatment.
2. **Minimum specifications:** There was the application of a very small number of rules or minimum specifications regarding the approach to treatment.
3. **Relationships:** There existed a complex web of relationships within the system, adapting and responding seemingly independently from each other.

Each of these three characteristics deserves additional consideration.

Agents

Peter was amazed at the number of medical personnel involved with his care: specialists, anesthesiologists, general surgeons, oncology surgeons, radiation oncologists, and, of course, the family physician. In addition, there were myriad others: dentists, nurses, radiation technicians, MRI and CT technologists, lab staff, speech and language therapists, and social workers. There were additional care professionals such as chiropractors, naturopaths, and spiritual care providers, as well as dozens of support and clerical staff. In complexity theory, these participants are called agents. They all worked and made decisions with their own subsystems (hospitals, clinical offices, treatment areas, etc.). Yet, they were all united in a common cause, and, rather than being driven from above, their work together served as a remarkable example of distributed leadership, communication, and trust. Certainly, a CEO and others in senior management were also involved, but there was no one in charge of this army of care providers who were all working in different settings and contexts with very different accountability structures. What they had in common were some inviolable commitments: optimizing the patient's experience, delivering the highest quality care for Peter as a unique patient, and making the best use of all available skills and technologies. They also had to deal with significant restraints. For example, radiation technology was evolving rapidly, so there was no standardized therapy. The technologists were adjusting just as quickly as everyone else.

Relationships between the various care providers were vital in terms of sharing information and making decisions that drew on their collective wisdom. A powerful change is happening in healthcare as the model of care moves from a hierarchical, physician-driven system to one that relies on interdisciplinary approaches that demand collaboration and very different skills. In most cases, a physician has primary accountability that manifests itself in the form of appropriate delegation, respectful consultation, and common values.

Every system is a vast network of many agents acting in parallel.[1] In the brain, the agents are nerve cells. In an anthill, the agents are the individual ants. And in an economy, the agents are individuals or households. In Peter's case, the agents were the various care providers. Each agent finds itself in the complex interactions with other agents, with each one acting in reacting in response to what they are experiencing. Hence the system is constantly adapting in highly unpredictable ways. Control is highly dispersed because of the localized nature of the responses. No one is in charge in the traditional sense. Despite the best efforts of those who would like to be in control, individuals, teams, and whole organizations seem to function from a place of enlightened self-interest. They make decisions in the moment based on what they are experiencing.

Systems are also highly complex in their structures, having many levels of organization. The individual agent is the simplest building block, but these individuals come together in very large systems of organization. For example, a nurse is an individual agent, but she or he is also part of a unit, which in turn is part of a department, which is part of a hospital, which is part of the healthcare system. Each level of organization is an agent, and the system is described as being nested within another system like a pile of ever-larger bowls in the kitchen cupboard. Systems are constantly revising and rearranging their building blocks as the individuals who make up the system gain experience. Be they individuals, teams, or hospitals, agents share common characteristics:

- **They act on local knowledge and conditions.** This means that a rich, two-way flow of information is vital to the capacity of the agents to expend their knowledge. Leaders who continue to see management-driven restructuring as their role and prerogative will be constantly fighting the system's capacity to organize itself in a manner that best suits its needs at the moment. When Peter organizes project groups in his classes, he provides them with three simple rules and then lets them select their own teammates based on their collective needs and individual decisions.[2]
- **They interact with one another based on specific rules of behavior.** These may be explicit, in the form of team norms, or they may be implicit, based on the evolving

culture of the system. These rules form the basis of "how we get things done around here." These rules need to be clear and worthwhile. When managers impose rules and policies with little or no value, or when the policies actually prevent the agents from working effectively, they will often find the agents working "behind management's back" in order to get things done.

- **They inspect one another's behaviors and then adjust their own as they learn and adapt.** Sometimes we need to learn that it is often the small movements of change that bring the largest shifts. Many large-scale change initiatives have been launched and had absolutely no impact.

Conversely, tiny changes can have dramatic effect. On December 1, 1955, in Montgomery, Alabama, Rosa Parks refused to obey the bus driver's order that she give up her seat in the "colored section" to a white passenger. This seemingly small action and the ensuing bus boycott became important symbols of the American Civil Rights movement: small action; large reaction.

Finally, an individual agent's response in the moment may in fact be triggered by something wholly unrelated to the situation in front of him or her. This is the power of the emotional centers of the brain where we hold our stories and emotional memories, and they are powerful triggers to action.

This understanding of how little changes and actions can have enormous change potential actually opens up the unique opportunity of each agent in the system to be the catalyst for change in the system. If you slowly pour out the contents of a pail of sand, a cone will form and, as the cone gets larger, landslides will occur. It is impossible to know when or exactly where, but one grain of sand can cause that tipping point[3] of change.

This understanding of the impact of small actions and their possibilities can also be incredibly empowering for the individual agents in the system. Their impact is commonly called the Butterfly Effect, which is based on a meteorologist's slightly tongue-in-cheek suggestion that "The flap of a butterfly's wings in Brazil could set off a tornado in Texas."[4] What the meteorologist discovered was that tiny changes at the beginning of a computerized simulation could have significant effect on the behavior of the system.

The critical action by leaders in these moments are to listen carefully to the people closest to a problem in order to hear their ideas, and then we need to support and encourage them to innovate. This means we need to develop a culture of safety where people are not punished when they try something new and it fails. Joel Barker encourages leaders to listen to the edges of an organization–that is, those places where there is more creativity and imagination–because those are the places that signal where the organization is going.[5] To be able to do so, leaders must create a place of safety where experimentation and even failure can take place. Each failure is a building block toward the eventual solution.

A CEO whom Peter admires is a huge proponent of this sort of approach. He has invested heavily in people at all levels of the organization, especially in the area of leadership development. At the beginning of each cohort of the new leadership program that the CEO directs, he candidly says:

> We have some big problems in this place – and some huge opportunities for positive change. If you think these answers are going to come from the executive offices, you will have a long wait. We are way too far from the action to know what's wrong, much less to know what to do about it. You are right there; you see it every day and you will come up with great solutions. Our job is to equip you in programs like this and to support you as you experiment. When you come up with ideas that could benefit the whole organization, then we also want to support you in finding ways to scale up the change. That's it. Have fun!

The CEO's statement has a remarkable impact on the people in the room. They see themselves as important contributors, not just as cogs in a wheel, and they are put in the place where they can succeed.

Participants in complex adaptive systems also need to become comfortable with a certain amount of uncertainty and ambiguity and not default to a policy manual for all their decisions. Such uncertainty and ambiguity can be disorienting initially, and there will be varying speeds of acclimatization. But if individuals and organizations are to thrive in this increasingly disorienting environment, they will need to recognize the need to let go of what has always been the way things were done.

Minimum Specifications

When Peter and Marion were planning their wedding, they reached the seemingly inevitable step of organizing the reception. Marion pulled out a large piece of paper and began drawing the circles that represented the tables in the hall. They had already agreed there would be no head table or speeches. After watching for a moment, Peter asked an absurd question: "What if, rather than masterminding the seating arrangements, we used a self-organizing approach?"

Marion had an immediate look of panic, but Peter pressed on. "How about this? When people arrive we tell them they can sit where they like but with just a few simple rules: First, sit where you like and if you don't like where you're sitting, move. Second, we'll have a host for each table whose job is to recruit guests so everyone feels wanted. And finally, we'll invite all the people who know absolutely no one but us to sit at our table. What do you think? It will be awesome!"

Marion's face perfectly reflected her terror at the prospect. As people are wont to do when presented with this sort of uncertainty, she immediately gravitated to a worst-case scenario. "But that will put [one of your family members] with my father – your family drinks too much and my father is a teetotaler. It will be a disaster!" She said this with the absolute certain knowledge it would happen, foreseeing the negative consequences.

With persistence Peter persuaded his bride to adopt the system. The results were hilarious. When people arrived looking for the seating chart, there was the predictable chaos and confusion. A request for more rules emerged, but then the table hosts went to work, and tables began to fill. Peter remembers Marion freezing beside him as she watched in horror as one of his family members approached the table of new in-laws. As this person approached the glassless table, he took in the barren landscape and slowed his steps. Then he suddenly veered to the right to a table with an abundance of glasses and sat down.

Peter gave Marion a mischievous look and said, "See, that's rule number one in action. Agents adapt to local knowledge and information!"

Marion laughed. "Only you would make my wedding a lesson in complexity theory."

This wedding story is an example of "minimum specifications" or "Min Specs." By specifying only the minimum number of simple rules, the Min Specs that must absolutely be respected, you can unleash a group to innovate freely.[6] Respecting the Min Specs will ensure that innovations will be both purposeful and responsible. Like the Ten Commandments or Christ's evocation of the *Shema* in Luke 10:27, Min Specs are enabling constraints: they detail only must do's and must not do's. When they are implemented, the clutter of nonessential rules, the Max Specs, that get in the way of innovation are eliminated.

This is where bureaucratic organizations such as denominations and long-established congregations are so vulnerable. Layers of processes and policies have evolved over the years. These layers require a navigational meandering where energy is spent simply on the navigational ability through the morass of rules and policies. Creativity and imagination are destroyed by the effort it takes to just navigate through the layers.

Institutions of higher education are layered in much the same way. Consequently they struggle to respond nimbly to the changing environment–for example, to challenges that confront them in the 21st century, challenges of fiscal responsibility and a changing student body of needs and expectations. Their systems and structures are unwieldy. Seminaries and universities unable or in some cases unwilling to reevaluate the processes and policies developed over the century will find themselves in crisis. They are already struggling with systems, structures, and attitudes that are no longer sustainable in the new world of economics and declining numbers. In some cases, they remain unaware or unwilling to acknowledge these realities. Creative new possibilities that would lead to more effective educational initiatives are at their fingertips. Accessibility and rhythms of learning, for example, have altered the educational landscape, but the university or seminary relentlessly marches to the rhythms of educational delivery that are convenient to the scholar teacher but not the student learner. One educational leader was heard to say, "We had a great opportunity to move into a more creative delivery system for our degree program, but we like the rhythms we have now." The resistance to change allows the morass of policies, governance systems, and decision-making committees to function in ways that filter out the creativity required to create a new possible future.

Often two to five Min Specs are sufficient to boost performance by adding more freedom and more responsibility to the group's understanding of what it must do to make progress. These are vital at organizational, team, and project levels. They help to define the space in which the group can self-organize. Added to the mission, values, and vision, they frame the way forward at an organizational level. At a project level, they help the group evaluate and decide what is absolutely essential for success. They open space for new possibilities, reduce frontline frustration, and free people from micromanagement. The Min Specs must be absolute. There can be no "yes, but."

One of Peter's clients uses Min Specs in a model they call "tight-loose-tight." Picture a vase that is smaller at the top and bottom than it is in the middle. At the top, the beginning, project specifications are clearly defined. For example, one project that Peter studied was focused on reducing wait times at the hospital. The Min Specs included three core commitments: reduction of wait times by 25 percent, a patient-centered approach, and optimizing value (best possible outcomes for the lowest possible cost). A multidisciplinary team of physicians, nurses, porters, and others was brought together, and they used Lean methodology[7] to generate dozens of possibilities, each of which they tried in a rapid cycle of quality strategies. All of this was fueled by immediate access to real-time data so the team could adjust.

All of these aspects–the experimentation, continuous feedback, failing/succeeding, and learning–were the loose parts of the process, or the middle section of the vase.

The bottom of the vase–that is, the other "tight" part–was the embedding of the approach the team developed into the functional processes of the organization and the ongoing monitoring of outcomes.

The role of the formal leaders in the organization was vital. They met with the project team weekly to encourage, support, and understand resource requirements. What they did not do was micromanage the process. As long as ideas were driven by the Min Specs, the team was encouraged to try them, and when some ideas failed, the encouragement to try other ideas continued. This approach is a radical shift in thinking for traditional managers who want to over specify (Max Specs) and manage the entire process. It takes time for both the formal leaders and the followers to adapt to the new environment, but the results will be worth it. In the example above, the project team far exceeded the 25 percent reduction initially expected, and those results, still monitored daily, have continued for four years now.

Relationships

Leadership is always relational. The quality of leadership is measured by its inherently relational and collegial process. It is a quality too often taken for granted. Margaret Wheatley put it well when she said, "Leadership is always dependent on the context but the context is established by the relationships we value."[8] If you want to know the effectiveness of a leader, you should ask the people who serve with her or him.

To be honest, there are no perfect assessments, psychological tests, or objective measures for what makes a leader effective. No model can perfectly determine that great leadership will follow. There are numerous examples of leaders who excelled in one environment and failed in another. Others of us can point to a leader who was average in one organization but, in moving to another organization, flew like an eagle. One of the explanations is that leadership is a relational skill. It is about fit and how you interact with others. There are situations in which we relate well. Other times, relationships are difficult. Nevertheless, whatever the situation, how we relate is directly connected to our effectiveness as a leader.

Gary remembers learning about the importance of relationship through an intervention by his mentor, George Baxter, in his first year out of seminary.[9] It is a lesson that has grounded his understanding of leadership.

One night, while deep asleep, Gary received a phone call from a couple from the church. Gary had been up to see their father in the hospital a couple of days before, and while he was aware of the father's cancer, Gary did not realize that these were the father's last days. In that late night phone call, family members told him that their father was in the last stages and would probably pass away in the next few hours. He thanked the couple for the call and told them that he would be up to the hospital first thing in the morning. He then hung up the phone and went back to sleep.

Fifteen minutes later, Gary's doorbell rang. Gary stumbled to the door, opened it, and was startled by the presence of the Senior Pastor–his colleague, friend, and mentor. George was obviously not happy and simply said, "Get dressed and come with me." Gary dressed quickly, curious as to what the issue was. He finally realized what was taking place when George pulled into the hospital parking lot. The two of them went up and found the family around the bed, some in tears, others in silence, obviously waiting as their father lived his last hours.

Gary remembers watching and participating as George cared for and comforted the different family members in the room with their dying father. It was like watching an artisan at work. After the father passed away and after seeing the family off home, George and Gary went to the car.

As George drove Gary home, very few words were spoken. Finally, George broke the silence. "Gary," he said, "these are the people you have been called to lead. Moments like these are the relational building blocks that will give you the credibility to do so. Moments like these will be remembered when you mess up. When people phone you to come to the hospital, you go!" His last comment to Gary that night was "If this ever happens again, it means you have not learned. And if it does happen again, you are fired!"

Relationships are absolutely key to this disorienting leadership we have been describing. We realize that relationship-building is natural for some and difficult for others, but there are some basic principles that can improve our ability to relate. Some of them are just common sense, and others are extremely challenging.

- **Express genuine care and concern**. Unless you are absolutely cold-hearted, you must have some amount of care for the people with whom you work. Genuinely putting those feelings into words is important. Try to understand the challenges. Listen! Leaders who take people seriously know when to stop talking and listen. It demands being willing to be fully present and ready to respond to whatever comes your way.
- **Establish and communicate high standards.** Most leaders struggle with this. They have personal expectations, but they may not be high standards. Even if they are high expectations, they are often not communicated well. Help people in the organization understand what success looks like and the level of excellence that the organization upholds.
- **Be open and encourage the perspective of others.** Ask people from all levels of the organization what their opinion is. As obvious as it may sound, leaders portray the fact they are actually interested in the views of others. Effective leaders are inclusive. They empower people who have ideas and points of view that are different.
- **Share relevant information.** Communicate! Communicate! Communicate! Be willing to give people the information they need to perform their job better. It may simply be the information they need to complete a task, or it may be keeping them in the loop so they know the background of the decisions that are being made. Go out of your way to be transparent and share information that will affect people so that they are not surprised when it does.
- **Model what you want to see.** You are always being watched. People will be attentive to what you do and how you do it. Modeling behavior will also establish behaviors within the organization or congregation.

- **Provide feedback clearly and candidly.** People need to know where they stand. This ability to clearly communicate combined with the ability to listen are skills that enable you to align people, decisions, and even agendas. Withholding your approval or disapproval comes across as a lack of engagement. Help others see that you are in fact engaged with them by responding to what they say, even nonverbally.
- **Relinquish the right to take offence.** Our colleague and friend, Janet Clark, holds this phrase as a principle of leadership.[10] She believes that when you take on a role of leadership, you simply relinquish the right to be offended by those who criticize and are hurtful with their words. It is not that leaders need to develop thick skin. The words may very well be personal, but as a leader, you choose not to give those words power. The speaker may very well need to be challenged or confronted, but not because your own personal feelings have been bruised.

To the above principles, we add the set of attitudes that Harlan Cleveland lists as indispensable to the management of complexity.[11] Leaders must have …

- A lively intellectual curiosity; an interest in everything– because everything really is related to everything else;
- A genuine interest in what other people think and why;
- A feeling of responsibility for envisioning an alternate future;
- A hunch that risks are not to be avoided;
- A mindset that crises are normal, tensions can be promising, and complexity is fun;
- A realization that paranoia and self-pity are reserved for people who don't want to lead;
- A sense of responsibility for outcomes;
- Unwarranted optimism and willingness to innovate.

These principles and attitudes, even in their simplicity, are extremely difficult to live out. We discuss them with individuals, groups, and organizations incessantly, and we have found that they are, unfortunately, not commonly practiced. To make them a part of your leadership style, these principles and attitudes require discipline in their use and consistent evaluation so that they become habits of heart.

Know Which Birdseed to Use

Complexity theory teaches that the organizational systems where people are involved to fulfill the mission are also the natural places in which change can take place. Knowing that people will move to the places to which they are naturally attracted, presenting the challenge as something they might solve will create fertile possibilities for change to take place. Once the change that needs to take place has been identified, the next step is to start identifying the key players, those whom you need in this initiative, and asking what would attract them to implement the needed change. This requires circling back and asking questions such as, "What would I have to do to make this idea as attractive to my stakeholders as possible? Am I willing to make the necessary adjustments to make it attractive to them?" The challenge of leadership is to articulate the attractions and frame them in the terms that will attract the people with whom you are working.

Daniel Pink, a brilliant motivational economist, did a meta-analysis of all the research on what drives human motivation. Pink's findings confirmed some surprising facts about the motivational factors that are required to cause people to work hard on a challenge.[12] Contrary to what an economist would tell us, one of the motivational factors is not money. Pink, through his studies, confirmed the carrot stick model of money as a motivating factor only works if you are looking for basic rudimentary tasks. If you want people to do simple things more efficiently and more effectively, paying the performance bonus works. But the minute you ask them to do more complex and algorithmic tasks where thinking is involved, people are not typically attracted by the bonus, and it actually causes them to perform less effectively.

So, if money does not motivate people, what does? Extensive research and practiced experience over the years has caused Peter to distill the factors into four powerful motivators. He refers to them as RAMP:

Relationships. Your relationships with the people in your organization provide you with the opportunity to pay attention to their individual self-interests. Self-interest is not a negative thing, and it does not require that you become a slave to the whims of your team. But becoming in-tune with people's self-interest involves taking the time to get to know your people and really listening to their concerns.

Autonomy. People want the chance to figure out matters on their own rather than be told explicitly how to do something. They want to be told the why, but not so much the how. Therefore, as a leader, coach your people where they need coaching and give feedback on what they are doing, but never micromanage. Give people the rationale and then allow them the autonomy to create the outcome.

Mastery. People need you to give them the time and space to get it right. Far too often we want to take over and say, "That's wrong. I'll fix it." This is one of the deadliest ways we can respond to mistakes.

Purpose. People deeply want to be connected to a higher purpose. In our leadership practice, we make sure we have early conversations with our teams about the why: Why are we doing this, why does this matter, and why does it matter to the organization as a whole? When people feel that they are an important contributor to the why, they are powerfully attracted. A few years ago, Simon Sinek spoke at a TED talk about the importance of starting with why.[13] In his presentation, Sinek explained that people do not buy what you are doing: they buy why you are doing it. If people believe they can rally around your higher purpose and values, then they will follow you.

Together, relationships, autonomy, mastery, and purpose remind us that our number one job as leaders is implementing these characteristics of motivational frames within the organizational cultures we lead.

Anticipate Resistance

The first question most people pose when we talk about the change process is generally framed around what we do with people who resist any change. It is a fair question and certainly one of the challenges of any organizational renewal.

"Change for change sake isn't always right you know!" Gary did not know why his colleague needed to tell him this in their morning discussion over coffee. It seemed important to her. They were discussing the changes occurring at the organization he was then leading. They wanted to position themselves as an organization for effective missions in the 21st century. The result had been a time of major transition in the structures, attitudes, and personnel. Change is never easy, and reframing an organization and refocusing good people who had been with the organization for years had made it all the more difficult.

Returning to his office, he found himself wondering why she felt the need to so emphatically state the truth about change. He had never seen himself as the kind of person who just needs to change things for the sake of shaking things up. Neither did he see himself as the kind of leader who forced change on others.

The truth was, she liked the organization the way it had been. To her, the organization's effectiveness was not as important as how comfortable she felt within the organization. New people meant that people like her would have to move over. Office shifts were inconvenient. Asking the question of "whether or not we could do this better?" was opening up a Pandora's Box of possible shifts she was unwilling to endure.

Robert Quinn in his book *Deep Change* tells us that change is not easy.[14] On first read, one wonders if he thought he was simply stating the obvious. However, change is never easy even if everyone in the room knows that it needs to take place. Birds are not naturally drawn to buckets.

While Peter was working in the healthcare system, he worked with the director of Women and Children's Health System. She had been convinced that the hospital needed to move to a postpartum and recovery model of care and support for women. In this new model, a woman could go into labor, give birth, and go through recovery and postpartum–all in the same room. Theoretically, this was a beautiful model. When the birth is normal, the model is reminiscent of the days in which all births took place at home.

Everybody on the team was on board to adopt this new model except for the most critical professionals in the room – the obstetricians. Without the support of the doctors whose job it was to deliver the babies, this change would never happen. To them, this change was out of the question.

One day, during a meeting with the team, Peter naively volunteered to investigate the problem. Not knowing much about the issue, he immediately went and chatted with two or three of the obstetricians. Within five minutes of their conversation, he found out that their dislike of the model was based on one thing. Obstetricians have the highest risk medical jobs in the province. They have more risk of being sued than any other physician in the hospital. In fact, they pay such massive insurance premiums that the government has to subsidize the cost. When these doctors looked at the initial plans and seeing that equipment for emergency cesareans had been removed and were farther away from the patient, they immediately considered the additional risk and the potential lawsuits. This was the deal-breaker for them. Once Peter realized this, he completely understood their dogged resistance.

Peter went back to the director and asked her if there was a chance of looking at reconfiguring the initial plan. She was adamant that the doctors were too resistant to the change and would never agree to the plan, even if it were modified. After hearing the concerns of the obstetricians, he thought this was strange. He went to the head of the department and explained the problem. Peter asked him if there was a way they could reconfigure the plan to satisfy the obstetricians. The department took one look at the plan and said "Sure," and proceeded to offer suggestions for how stations and equipment could be rearranged. By the end of the day, Peter came away with a plan for the new model that not only reduced the risk of lawsuit for the obstetricians but also was an overall improvement on the initial plan. The whole team was happy and embraced the new model.

The director of Women and Children's Health System took a resistive approach to change that is all too common. She was so busy trying to overcome the obstetricians' resistance that she could not make the mental flip to ask, "How do I understand their needs to make this an attraction?"

People who take a traditional approach to change management consistently focus on how to overcome change resistance. The reality is that change resistance is exhausting for everybody and is captive to a mechanistic mindset. To move from a mechanistic mindset to one that sees things more relationally and organically takes a great effort. Leaders who move to a more relational organic style are constantly looking for the win-win situation as a motivating factor.

In physical terms, resistance happens when one solid object meets another, rubs against it, and creates friction. Once we imagine resistance in these terms, we can clearly see that overcoming resistance is a matter of increasing traction, using the friction to generate forward movement. In Peter's case, overcoming resistance to change at the hospital required leveraging the friction between the interests of the obstetricians and the rest of the team to develop an even better plan for change.

If you want bumblebees in your garden, you had better plant flowers that attract bumblebees. Once you do that, you will hopefully get all the bumblebees you would ever want and can even avoid getting stung in the process. When the team at the hospital shifted their thinking to how to focus on attracting people to change rather than assuming they would have to fight to overcome resistance, they ended up with a beautiful layout with centralized emergency and happier people.

Peter has lost count of how many times he has used this interpretation of the "birds and the bees" metaphor with physicians and pastors. When he does, the light goes on with respect to the challenges they are facing and the strategies they have employed to address them. They realize, "That's what I've been doing all along." And they realize how much it is wearing them out.

Be Prepared to Lose a Few Birds

Once leaders of churches, hospitals, and other complex organizations understand the importance of attractors and creating traction out of resistance in leading change, there is still a question that lingers in the back of their minds: "How do we get everybody on board?" The question assumes that if you do not get everybody to embrace the change, change will not occur. Leaders who think this way automatically conjure up the worst-case scenarios of resistance. For pastors, the worst case could be that group that has been in the church forever and gives a lot of money but hates change.

Resistance theory elicits a much more optimistic picture of change. It frames change in the visual image of a bell curve. In the beginning of the process toward change, a lot of effort is required, but eventually a tipping point takes place that moves the organization toward the change being proposed. Once that tipping point is reached, everything seems to take off. This is where the most important learning takes place and when a critical mass of people gets on board. While most people assume that change happens when 100 percent, or at least 50 percent plus one get on board, research shows that only 30 to 35 percent of people constitutes critical mass. In fact, 100 percent buy-in of the proposed changes is unhealthy for the system because it means your organization is back into the position of excessive stability and homeostasis. Instead, what you want is that critical mass of people moving toward the change while others are still resisting and creating tension.

Gary remembers the time he was serving a church early in his career. In a conversation with the secretary who had served the church for over 30 years, he described his idea to remodel a particular meeting room. After he had made his pitch for the change, she looked at him with studied seriousness and said with wry simplicity, "I have seen that room painted nine different colors and have witnessed the furnishings rearranged each time. I have also seen pastors come and go!" It was obvious that she was one of many people in the congregation who would not resist change but also would not get excited about it. These are people you will find in any organization. They, along with other groups within complex organizations, whether they be businesses, nonprofit development agencies, churches, or hospitals, can be roughly divided into four groups:

- **The "Yes!" people**. About 10 percent at the front end of proposed changes are the early adapters. These are the people who immediately respond to change with, "Yes, we love it!" And they love it for many different reasons. These are the people who need to be identified early on. They can help win over the more hesitant, resistant groups.
- **The "Yes, if ..." people**. In addition to the 10 percent who say "Yes!", there typically are 15 percent who say, "Yes, if ...?" Many leaders misinterpret this group as part of the opposition, but it is not. This group simply needs more clarification and communication. These people want a little more detail, structure, communication, and understanding of how people might be affected by this change. Ultimately, this group is hesitant, but not resistant to change.
- **The "No, because ..." people**. The real resistance comes from the 15 percent who sit at the back end and offer variations of "No, because ...." They are the ones who will use phrases such as "Let me play devil's advocate," or "No, we've tried that before and it won't work." Being aware of this group and working to understand why they are opposed to change will allow the integration of their questions into the plan. These are also the people who tend to drain the leader's emotional energy, especially if their questions cannot be answered quickly. Sometimes, they are also the people who actually do not want answers. They are really just naysayers who have the potential to sap the leader dry if too much energy is put into assuaging their concerns.
- **The "Whatever" people**. In the middle of the bell curve, you have 50 percent who are saying, "Yeah, whatever. I don't care." They are the ones who use phrases like "This is the program of the week. It's not my problem." In a congregation, it can be closer to 90 percent of the

people who say "Whatever. I just show up on Sunday." The measure of the health of a church is the size of its "Whatever" group – the lower its size, the healthier the church. The naysayers in the back end and the "Yes!" people in the front end are both expected. It is the size of the apathetic group that determines the health of the church.

The leader's job is to articulate the direction and use clear language to describe the attractors. Focus first on equipping and educating the 10 percent who say "Yes!" so they become the first followers. They can be the people who work with the 15 percent who are saying "Yes, but …" to encourage them to move forward. Then, those in front of the apathetic group of 50 percent will start paying attention to the energy and say, "Hmm, this may not be so bad." The last group to engage will always be the last group that says "No, because …." They can be asked "Is this change a deal-breaker? If so, how might your concern be addressed?"

Above all, the most critical question for the leader is "Where am I going to invest my emotional energy?" If we invest it in the back end on the naysayers, as we historically have done, we will get exactly what they offer – resistance. If we want validation, encouragement, and support, we leaders must focus our energy on the people who want to go where we believe they need to go. This does not mean that we ignore or undermine the people at the back end, but it does mean not allowing the naysayers to hijack the process. They cannot be allowed to take over meetings. Leaders in moments like that will often use questions such as "Can we talk about this offline?" to avoid those possibilities. Another strategy is to work to move the change forward by expressing both understanding and confident direction with a statement such as "Let me understand your specific needs as we move forward in this direction." It takes courage not to back down from opposition. At the same time, it takes courage to attempt to discover how you can incorporate that resistance into where you are going.

We believe and have experienced that focusing our emotional energy at the front of the bell curve is a freeing experience. Peter has people tell him this all the time. It is like a declaration of independence. The shift of focus frees the leader from fretting and fussing about those who hate the change to focusing his or her energy on the people who are passionately committed.

Steve Holmes is the chair of the board of governors of Tyndale and is perhaps one of the truest entrepreneurs either of us has ever met. As President of SpringFree Trampolines and VerifEye Technologies, he has a varied portfolio of business enterprises. He is known for the freewheeling yet intentional ways in which he leads his organizations. As they implement change in the industries in which he is focused, he often asks these four questions:

1. What is the best thing that could happen if we do this?
2. What is the worst thing that could happen if we do this?
3. What is the best thing that could happen if we do not do this?
4. What is the worst thing that could happen if we do not do this?

The discussion among his management team in response to these four questions evokes clear thinking and brings issues to the surface. Ultimately, this discussion leads to more informed decision-making.

Let the Birds Fly

Knowing that we do not need to get everybody on board in order for change to happen allows the leader to adopt a far more organic approach to leading the organization. Leading change starts by communicating what we are doing and why we are doing it. It provides the atmosphere in which people can be invited to dance if they want to dance. It also gives people permission not to dance as long as they are not undermining the way forward.

Lately the phrase "If you're not on the bus, you're off the bus" has come into vogue. This has emerged from Jim Collins' metaphor and statement on leadership's task of "making sure the right people are on the bus."[15] It is catchy and clear but may be dangerous if the leaders assume that having the right people on the bus means unanimity of opinion. Instead, we propose to clarify some aspects of the metaphor:

- Figure out where the bus is going.
- Let people know where it is going.
- Invite those who want to go there to go from the beginning.
- Let people know that this bus is not on an express route.

The bus will make multiple stops. Those who get picked up on route to our destination should be welcomed as if they were there from the beginning. In short, we need to have the grace and the mercy to let people take their time to get on the bus, and if they choose not to, have the grace and mercy to let them get off. This implies that rather than trying to force people to get on the bus, we say "Okay, I completely understand that this is not where you want to go. How can I help you find the place you want to go?"

The parable found in Matthew 20:1–16 offers insight into the idea that not everybody needs to be on board at the same time. Many of us have found it frustrating to understand the fairness of the landowner who hires workers at different times of the day and in the end pays them all the same amount. The final few verses elicit the feeling most of us have in response to the parable:

> When evening came, the owner of the vineyard said to his supervisor, "Call the workers and pay them their wages, beginning with the last ones hired and going on to the first." The workers who were hired about five in the afternoon came and each received a denarius. So, when those came who were hired first, they expected to receive more. But each one of them also received a denarius. When they received it, they began to grumble against the landowner. "These who were hired last worked only one hour," they said, "and you have made them equal to us who have borne the burden of the work and the heat of the day." But he answered one of them, "Friend, I am not being unfair to you. Didn't you agree to work for a denarius? Take your pay and go. I want to give the one who was hired last the same as I gave you. Don't I have the right to do what I want with my own money? Or are you envious because I am

generous?" So the last will be first, and the first will be last. (vv. 8–16, TNIV)

The parable challenges our views on what the reward for servanthood looks like. In the context of our discussion on change, a person's value to the organization is not about when the person joined the process. A healthy organization allows for people to join and enter in at various stages without penalty and with the same reward – being part of a healthy organization or congregation.

Having this perspective is a strategic and wholesome way of entering into change. It is an initiative that reflects the leader's ability to see change as an ongoing process and not simply as a one-off decision. We have seen life and dynamic mission emerge in congregations and organizations as a result of adopting the perspective that the organization is not an express bus.

Peter's home church has experienced this first hand. The emergence of a more theologically conservative church in their area caused some people to move to the new church. They felt more attuned to this new congregation's predictability and sureness. Rather than trying to fight the change and coerce people not to leave, the leadership chose to live differently amidst the shifts that were taking place. While they mourn the loss that comes with change, they have acknowledged that some people are not attracted to the more open yet evangelical ethos that their own church promotes. They demonstrated that they are not trying to be the church for everybody. In sticking to their sense of purpose, mission, and values in the midst of change, they reinvited their people to become an active part of the church.

Leadership, as opposed to treating people like parts of a machine, is about capturing people's discretionary energy. It is using essential attractors to motivate people to give you the best of what they have instead of just showing up and doing their job.

Bringing It All Together

The challenge of getting our people "to the bucket" is the challenge of leadership. We have discussed the incredible shifts taking place on our globe. We have considered the character and trajectory of servant leadership as being the kind of leadership required for this time. We have challenged the views we hold on organizations, shifting our metaphorical perspective on how we look at organizations from a mechanistic to an organic image. For the church, we believe the organic image aligns with some of Christ's own metaphors – the vine and the branches, for example. We have also discussed how real change happens (emergent and bottom up) and especially how that takes place in the reality of organizations that are complex adaptive systems. Finally, we mapped out the transformational leadership task.

Throughout the book, we have woven a thread that explores a leadership model in which the leader is not so much the knight on a white horse charging into battle with his troops arrayed in rank and file behind him, but have instead presented leadership as it focuses on mobilizing all members of the organization to make conscious decisions about where each needs to be and which role each needs to play in the system. Certainly there are times when the system needs the leader out in front, but more often organizations need the leader working side-by-side or even from the rear, offering encouragement and support as members of the system self-organize around ideas and opportunities of their own making – all in pursuit of a common purpose. This is transformational servant leadership–an idea reaching back at least as far as the teachings of Jesus, yet an idea ripe for our times.

7

"It's All about Relationships"

Peter Vaill, one of today's leading thinkers and practitioners of organizational development, was one of Peter's professors when he worked on his doctoral degree. One day in a conversation with Peter, Vaill commented that "healthcare had been the 'canary in the mine shaft'" when it came to the changes and challenges that business leaders were beginning to face in the 21st century. Healthcare simply had to face the issues much sooner. His concluding remark has stayed with Peter: "Others are just waking up to the reality of what's happening."

Vaill's assessment offers a fitting conclusion to what we have been arguing in this book. If the healthcare profession was "the canary in the mine shaft," we wonder if the church has been the ostrich with its head in the sand. The signs and disorienting dilemmas have been happening all around her. In one sense, they have been difficult to miss. In another sense, the church has simply ignored them. We love the church, and we have both dedicated our lives to its nurture and life. But we who are in the church have to get our heads out of the sand. We have to move beyond insider conversations that get deeper into theological mind games and further from true implementation and change.

Gary sits as a guest on a denominational body's missional task force. He listens to the conversations, saddened at how unaware people are of the deep shifts taking place in society and religious life. Competent leaders appear oblivious to how gravely we lack connection with the communities outside the walls of our churches. This is not surprising. If you are a denomination, local church, or other kind of organization with significant endowments, you are able live in the illusion of security, equating health with solid finances. But the world has changed, and it continues to do so. Predictability and sureness have gone out the window. Circumstances can change on a dime. This is the reality of the complex world in which we live today. This is why Westley, Zimmerman and Patton write,

> Complexity science embraces life as it is: unpredictable, emergent, evolving and adaptable–not the least bit machine like. And though it implies that even though we can't control the world in the way we can control a machine, we are not powerless either. Using insights about how the world is changed, we can become active participants in shaping those changes.[1]

Those who struggle to make a difference or create change face two truths. The first is that success or effectiveness is not a fixed address. The second is that failure can open the way to success, so it is better to try something and fail than not to try anything at all. This unpredictability requires courageous leadership that is adaptable and nimble in its task.

The circumstances that have shaped the writing of this book offer an apt illustration of this. After signing our contract with Chalice Press, Peter and I met to outline the tasks that would get us to the finished manuscript. Within a week of that meeting, Peter's health took a turn for the worse. Complications from his cancer treatment nine years previous had caused the bone in his jaw to decay and become infected. The pain was excruciating, and drug treatment severely handicapped his ability to think and write. After lengthy considerations, the decision was made to try an innovative procedure – a jaw implant.

Recounting the details of the months that led up to the procedure and Peter's still ongoing recovery would take many pages. Suffice it to say, this circumstance portrays the unpredictability of life. It is an illustration of complex systems at work. Required deadlines were intertwined with unpredictable conditions and unanticipated circumstances. We talked a lot. We listened a lot. We devised alternative plans to accomplish the writing goals we had set. We employed strategies of nimbleness, flexibility, and the ability to bring relationships around us to work within our particular circumstances. It has been a time of uncertainty.

We suggest that it is this complexity and uncertainty that offers the greatest possibility for transformation. Settling in and simply working harder doing the things we have always done will not produce the possible solutions to the challenges we face. These actions may stem the tide for a while, but only for the most securely insulated organizations whose competition or circumstances are less vulnerable than others. Whether the challenge be congregational renewal or organizational health, avoiding change is not an option, and facing the challenges head on must be embraced.

Getting comfortable with acting in the face of uncertainty is part of the adventure. Mary Jo Leddy, the Catholic theologian and refugee activist in an address given to members of the Salvation Army, spoke prophetically when she proclaimed, "The future belongs to those who have nothing to lose."[2] We would do well to remember this. Innovation and change are as much about letting go as they are about taking control. Innovation is framed in the courageous initiative to move forward. Freedom to fail is as much about change as coming up with the right solutions. Clutching and grasping on to what was will only lead to decay in organizations. Sometimes action will precede knowledge, and in the acting, understanding will emerge.

The principles and foundational understandings we have presented here do not promise success. They do, however, provide the conditions in which leadership and organizational health are possible. In their book *Getting to Maybe,* Brenda Zimmerman, France Westley and Michael Quinn Patton state it well. Embracing these principles at least tip the "scales in favor of successful social innovations in the face of seemingly overwhelming odds."[3]

We have espoused a transformational servant leadership that calls for leaders to give people space, to respect them in such a way that we let them think, create, experiment, and even fail. It calls for leaders to step back and fight every inner impulse to want to control and box things up neatly because, in fighting that urge, they will allow solutions to emerge. It calls us to take relationships seriously because it is in the complexity of relationships that answers will be discovered.

Gary met with his former mentor, George Baxter, just a week before we finished the manuscript for this book.[4] It had been a few years since they last met, so there was some catching up to do. They had a wonderful time of conversation and reflection. They laughed about old times together. They reflected on what was happening in the world. Mostly, they reminisced about times they had worked and learned together.

At one point in the conversation, they talked about leadership. Gary thanked him for his role in shaping his life and leadership. George summed up leadership so well. "Gary, leadership is not that difficult, and effective leadership is not that complicated. You can't control the situation or the circumstances, but you can control the way you deal with them. It doesn't matter what decade you are in, leadership is all about relationships. It's all about relationships." George is right.

Notes

Chapter 1: Re-Imagining Leadership

[1]Jim Collins, "The Misguided Mix up of Celebrity and Leadership," Conference Board Annual Report, Annual Feature Essay, http://www.jimcollins.com/article_topics/articles/the-misguided-mixup.html.

[2]Gary V. Nelson, *Borderland Churches: A Congregation's Introduction to Missional Living* (St. Louis: Chalice Press, 2008).

[3]Joshua Cooper Ramo, *The Age of the Unthinkable: Why the New World Disorder Constantly Surprises Us and What We Can Do About It* (Boston: Little, Brown & Company, 2010).

[4]Ibid., 260.

[5]Jean Lipman-Blumen, *Connective Leadership: Managing in a Changing World* (New York: Oxford University Press, 1996), 6.

[6]James Hunter, *The World's Most Powerful Leadership Principle* (New York: Crown Publishing Group, 2004), 45.

[7]Brian Craig, Director of Leadership Development, Canadian Baptists of Ontario and Quebec.

[8]Tim Keel, *Intuitive Leadership: Embracing a Paradigm of Narrative, Metaphor, and Chaos* (Grand Rapids: Baker Books, 2009), 117.

[9]Reggie McNeal, *Practicing Greatness: 7 Disciplines of Extraordinary Spiritual Leaders* (San Francisco: Jossey-Bass, 2006).

[10]Vaclav Havel, "The New Measure of Man," *New York Times* (July 8, 1994).

[11]Peter Senge, "Communities of Leaders and Learners," The 75th anniversary issue of *Harvard Business Review* (September-October, 1997).

[12]Margaret Wheatley, *Finding our Way: Leadership for an Uncertain Time* (San Francisco: Berrett-Koehler, 2005), 56.

[13]Jack Mezirow, *Learning as Transformation* (San Francisco: Jossey-Bass, 2000).

[14]Ramo, *Age of the Unthinkable*, 11.

[15]Jaroslav Pelikan, interview with *U.S. News & World Report*, July 26, 1989. (The interview focused on his book *The Vindication of Tradition* (New Haven, Conn.: Yale University Press, 1986).)

[16]Peter Senge, *Leading Learning Organizations: The Bold, the Powerful, and the Invisible* (San Francisco: Jossey-Bass, 1996), 45.

Chapter 2: From Kirk to Picard

[1]See Leonard Hjalmarson, http://www.nexuscentre.ca/files/kingdomleadership_8.pdf.

[2]Warren Bennis, G.M. Spreitzer and T.G. Cummings, eds., *The Future of Leadership* (San Francisco: Jossey-Bass, 2001).

[3]S. M. Bornstein, and A.F. Smith, "The puzzles of leadership." In *The Leader of the Future: New Visions, Strategies, and Practices for the Next Era*, ed. F. Hesselbein, M. Goldsmith, and R. Beckhard (San Francisco: Jossey-Bass, 1996), 281–92.

[4]Joseph C. Rost, *Leadership for the Twenty-First Century* (New York: Praeger, 1991), 487.

[5]Jim Collins http://www.jimcollins.com/article_topics/articles/the-misguided-mixup.html.

[6]Robert K. Greenleaf, *The Servant as Leader* (Westfield, Ind., and Atlanta: Robert Greenleaf Centre, 1982).

[7]Robert K. Greenleaf, R. K., *Servant-leadership: A Journey into the Nature of Legitimate Power and Greatness* (Mahwah, N.J.: Paulist Press), 27.

⁸Simon Sinek, *Leaders Eat Last* (New York: Portfolio Penguin, 2014).

⁹William Willimon, Banff Pastor's Conference, 1992.

¹⁰Richard Foster, *Celebration of Discipline,* 3d ed. (San Francisco: Harper, 2002), 132.

¹¹Henri Nouwen, *In the Name of Jesus: Reflections on Christian Leadership* (London: St. Paul's Press, 1989), 82.

¹²Ibid.

¹³Dallas Willard, *The Spirit of the Disciplines* (New York: Harper Collins, 1988), 183.

¹⁴Ibid.

¹⁵James Macgregor Burns, *Leadership* (New York: Harper & Row, 1978, reprinted 2010).

¹⁶M. Wheatley, *Leadership and the New Science* (San Francisco: Berrett-Koehler 1994); B. Zimmerman, C. Lindberg and P. Plsek, *Edgeware* (Irving, Tex.: VHA 1998); S. Kelly and M. Allison, *The Complexity Advantage* (New York: McGraw-Hill, 1998).

¹⁷Max De Pree, "The Measure of Leadership," *Theology, News & Notes* (Fuller Theological Seminary: Spring 2014), 41.

¹⁸Alan Roxburgh, *The Missional Leader: Equipping Your Church to Reach a Changing World* (San Francisco: Jossey-Bass, 2008), 145.

¹⁹For a helpful resource on leadership see, Max De Pree, *Leadership is an Art* (New York: Doubleday, 1989).

²⁰Charles Van Engen, *God's Missionary People: Rethinking the Purpose of the Local Church* (Grand Rapids: Baker Books, 1991), 165.

²¹Sinek, *Leaders Eat Last*, 214.

²²Quoted in Richard J. Neuhaus, *Freedom for Ministry* (New York: Harper & Row, 1992), 13.

²³Sinek, *Leaders Eat Last*, 18.

²⁴See https://www.greenleaf.org/what-is-servant-leadership.

Chapter 3: Re-Visioning the Organizations We Lead

¹Roger von Oech, *A Kick in the Seat of the Pants* (New York: William Morrow Paperbacks, 1986), and *A Whack on the Side of the Head* (New York: Harper & Row, 1992), 167.

²Von Oech, *A Whack*, 167.

³Neil Postman & Charles Weingartner, *Teaching as a Subversive Activity* (New York: Dell Publishing, 1969).

⁴Von Oech, *A Kick*, 26.

⁵See George Lakoff and Mark Johnson, *Metaphors We Live By* (Chicago: University of Chicago Press , 2003).

⁶Avery Dulles, *Models of the Church* (New York: Image Books, 1991).

⁷Gareth Morgan, *Images of Organizations* (Thousand Oaks, Calif.: Sage, 2006).

⁸See Fredrick Taylor, *The Principles of Scientific Management* (New York: Harper & Brothers, 1911; reprinted by New York: Cosimo Classics, 2006).

⁹A term created by Tom Burns and G.M. Stalker in the late 1950s. See T. Burns and G.M. Stalker, *The Management of Innovation* (London: Tavistock, 1961) and, for church and congregations, see N. Cole, *Organic Church: Growing Faith Where Life Happens* (San Francisco: Jossey-Bass, 2005).

¹⁰Malcolm Gladwell, *The Tipping Point: How Little Things Can Make a Big Difference* (New York: Bay Back Books, 2002).

¹¹Andrew S. Grove, *Only the Paranoid Survive: How to Exploit the Crisis Points That Challenge Every Company and Career* (New York: Currency/Doubleday, 1996).

¹²Ibid.

¹³Ibid., 68.

¹⁴Jim Collins, *How the Mighty Fall* (Jim Collins Services, 2009).

[15]See http://www.jimcollins.com/books/how-the-mighty-fall.html.

[16]Ron Ashkenas, *The Organization of the Future* (San Francisco: Jossey-Bass, 1997), 105.

[17]See http://www.slideshare.net/bright9977/25-management-lessons-from-peter-drucker-7109567.

[18]Max De Pree, *Leadership is an Art* (East Lansing, Mich.: Michigan State University Press, 1987; reprint, New York: Crown Business, 2004).

[19]Peter Senge, *The Fifth Discipline: The Art and Practice of the Learning Organization* (New York: Random House, 1990), 353.

[20]Ibid., 358.

[21]Ibid., 344.

[22]Ibid., 345.

[23]Ibid., 351.

[24]Peter Block, *Stewardship: Choosing Service over Self-Interest* (San Francisco: Berrett-Koehler, 2013).

[25]Susan Howatch, *Absolute Truths* (New York: Knopf, 1995).

Chapter 4: What Has Changed about Change

[1]Edwin Olson and Glenda Eoyang, *Facilitating Organization Change: Lessons from Complexity Science* (San Francisco: Jossey-Bass, 2001).

[2]Ronald Heifetz, *Leadership without Easy Answers* (Cambridge, Mass.: Belknap Press, 1994).

[3]Brenda Zimmerman, Curt Lindberg, and Paul Plsek, *Edgeware: Insights from Complexity Science for Health Care Leaders* (Irving, Tex.: VHA Inc, 1998).

[4]See more at: http://learningforsustainability.net/sparksforchange/complicated-or-complex-knowing-the-difference-is-important-for-the-management-of-adaptive-systems/#sthash.DdLwdnm4.dpuf.

[5]See more at: http://learningforsustainability.net/sparksforchange/complicated-or-complex-knowing-the-difference-is-important-for-the-management-of-adaptive-systems/#sthash.DdLwdnm4.dpuf.

[6]Paul Plsek and T. Greenhalgh, "Complexity science: The challenge of complexity in health care," *British Medical Journal* (Sept 15: 323[7313], 2001), 625–28.

[7]Holden, "Complex Adaptive Systems: Concept Analysis," *Journal of Advanced Nursing* 52, no. 6, (2005): 651–57.

[8]Plowman, Solansky, Beck, Kulkarne, and Travis, "The role of leadership in emergent, self-organization," *Leadership Quarterly* 18, no. 4 (2007): 341–56.

[9]Mitchell Waldrop, *Complexity: The Emerging Science on the Edge of Order and Chaos* (New York: Touchstone, 1992), 184.

[10]Ibid., 278.

[11]H.J.J. Lanham, R.R. McDaniel, B.F. Crabtree, W.L. Miller, K.C. Stange, and A.F. Tallia, "How improving practice relationships among clinicians and nonclinicians can improve quality in primary care," *The Joint Commission on Quality and Patient Safety* 35, no. 9 (2009): 457–66.

[12]See http://c.ymcdn.com/sites/www.plexusinstitute.org/resource/collection/6528ED29-9907-4BC78D008DC907679FED/ComplicatedAndComplexSystemsZimmermanReport_Medicare_reform.pdfZimmerman.

[13]P. Rost, *Leadership for the 21st Century* (Westport, Conn.: Praeger, 1993), 102.

[14]Claire Lindberg, Sue Nash and Curt Lindberg, *On the Edge: Nursing in the Age of Complexity* (Bordentown, N.J.: Plexis Institute, 2008).

[15]See http://digitalcommons.unl.edu/cgi/viewcontent.cgi?article=1066&context=managementfacpb 2007, 343.

[16]Ronald A. Heifetz & Donald L. Laurie, "The Work of Leadership," *Harvard Business Review* (December 2001).

[17]Margaret Wheatley, "Goodbye Command and Control," in *Leader to Leader* (July 1997).

Chapter 5: The Task: Leading Transformationally

[1]See http://www.management-issues.com/opinion/1125/the-difference-between-management--leadership/.

[2]See http://mindsetmatters.com.au/Portals/0/dox/what%20leaders%20really%20do%20j%20kotter.pdf.

[3]K. B. Lowe & W. L. Gardner, "Ten years of *The Leadership Quarterly*: Contributions and challenges for the future," *The Leadership Quarterly* 11, no. 4 (2001): 648–57.

[4]Bernard Bass and Bruce Avilio, *Improving Organizational Effectiveness* (Thousand Oaks, Calif.: Sage, 1994).

[5]Ibid.

[6]See http://www.theglobeandmail.com/globe-debate/move-over-hillary-elizabeths-a-contender/article19395229/.

[7]See http://humaneeducation.org/blog/2013/02/18/clear-values-%E2%89%A0-easy-decisions/.

[8]Edgar Schein, *Organizational Culture and Leadership: A Dynamic View* (San Francisco: Jossey-Bass, 1992).

[9]Edwin Friedman, *A Failure of Nerve: Leadership in an Age of the Quick Fix* (New York: Church Publishing, Inc, 2007), 13.

[10]Gordon MacDonald, *Building below the Waterline: Strengthening the Life of a Leader* (Boston: Hendricksonn, 2011, reprinted 2013), 13.

[11]See Lee Bolman and Terence Deal, *Leading with Soul: An Uncommon Journey of Spirit*, 3d ed. (San Francisco: Jossey-Bass, 2011) and Lance Secretan, *Reclaiming Higher Ground: Creating Organizations that Inspire the Soul* (Toronto: Macmillan Canada, 1997).

[12]Jim Clemmer, *Growing the Distance: Timeless Principles for Personal, Career, and Family Success* (Toronto: TCG Press, 1999), 105.

[13]Discussion with Brian Craig, Director of Leadership Development, Canadian Baptists of Ontario and Quebec.

[14]Jimmy Long, *Emerging Hope: A Strategy for Reaching Postmodern Generations* (Downers Grove, Ill.: InterVarsity Press, 2004), 99.

Chapter 6: The Rock, The Bird, and the Bucket

[1]M. Mitchell Waldrop, *Complexity: The Emerging Science at the Edge of Order and Chaos* (New York: Simon & Schuster, 1993), 145.

[2]In a typical class of 20 to 24, I want teams of 6 to 8 members. Before they form teams, they each do a "wanted poster" for themselves that indicates their name, department or discipline, key strengths (i.e., why others would want you), and team needs (i.e., what you want from others). These posters are then hung up for all to see. Then I indicate that we need three teams and the rules are: (1) the teams must be roughly equal in number, (2) they should leverage strengths (based on the posters), and (3) they should leverage interdependence (i.e., not all from one department or discipline). There is typically a brief period of chaos and wandering about, with predictable levels of comprehension, fear, and confusion. Then individuals come together and teams form, typically within 4 to 5 minutes. By using this process, there is no master control or manipulation (from me), and it is the participants' first introduction to a self-organizing system.

[3]See Malcolm Gladwell, *Tipping Point: How Little Things Can Make a Big Difference* (New York: Back Bay Books, 2002).

[4]See http://www.stsci.edu/~lbradley/seminar/butterfly.html.

[5]See Joel Barkers, *Future's Edge: Discovering the New Paradigms of Success* (New York: William Morrow, 1992).

[6]For more information on how to develop Min Specs with a group, refer to www.liberatingstructures.com, an excellent collection of facilitation approaches that support emergent change.

[7]See Lean methodology of Quality/process improvement methodology first developed by Toyota described in James Womack, Daniel Roos and Daniel Jones, *The Machine that Changed the World* (New York: Productivity Press, 1990).

[8]Margaret Wheatley, *Leadership and the New Science* (San Francisco: Berrett-Koehler, 1992), 144.

[9]George Baxter, Minister Emeritus, First Baptist Church, Regina, Saskatchewan.

[10]Janet Clark, Senior Vice President of Academics and Dean of the Seminary, Tyndale University College & Seminary.

[11]Harlan Cleveland, *Nobody in Charge: Essays on Leadership* (San Francisco: Jossey-Bass, 2002), 96.

[12]Daniel Pink, *Drive: The Surprising Truth about What Motivates Us* (New York: RiverHead, 2009; reprint, New York: River Trade Books, 2011). See also https://www.youtube.com/watch?v=_mG-hhWL_ug.

[13]See https://www.youtube.com/watch?v=sioZd3AxmnE.

[14]Robert Quinn, *Deep Change: Discovering the Leader Within* (San Francisco: Jossey Bass, 1996).

[15]Jim Collins, *Good to Great: Why Some Companies Make the Leap… and Others Don't* (New York: Harper Business, 2001).

Chapter 7: "It's All about Relationships"

[1]Francis Westley, Brenda Zimmerman, Michael Quinn Patton, *Getting to Maybe: How the World Has Changed* (Toronto: Vintage Canada, 2007), 7.

[2]Address given to the National Salvation Army Staff at the Delta Hotel, Mississauga, Ontario, November, 2001.

[3]Westley, Zimmerman, Patton, *Getting to Maybe*, 7.

[4]George Baxter, Minister Emeritus, First Baptist Church, Regina, Saskatchewan.

CPSIA information can be obtained
at www.ICGtesting.com
Printed in the USA
FFOW03n1810130415
12594FF